ORELA Protecting Studen
Civil Rights in the
Educational Environment

Teacher Certification Exam

M000276958

By: Sharon Wynne, M.S.

XAMonline, INC.

Boston

XAMonline, Inc.
25 First Street Suite 106
Cambridge, MA 02141
Toll Free 1-800-509-4128
Email: info@xamonline.com
Web www.xamonline.com
Fax: 1-617-583-5552

Library of Congress Cataloguing-in-Publication Data

Wynne, Sharon A.
    ORELA: Protecting Students and Civil Rights Teacher Certification / Sharon A. Wynne. -1st ed.

ISBN: 978-1-60787-173-6
1. Civil Rights in Education.   2. Study Guides.   3. ORELA.
4. Teachers' Certification & Licensure.   5. Careers.

Disclaimer:
The opinions expressed in this publication are the sole works of XAMonline and were created independently from the National Education Association, Educational Testing Service, or any State Department of Education, National Evaluation Systems or other testing affiliates.

Between the time of publication and printing, state specific standards as well as testing formats and website information may change that is not included in part or in whole within this product. Sample test questions are developed by XAMonline and reflect content similar to that on real tests; however, they are not former tests. XAMonline assembles content that aligns with state standards but makes no claims nor guarantees teacher candidates a passing score. Numerical scores are determined by testing companies such as NES or ETS and then are compared with individual state standards. A passing score varies from state to state.

ORELA: Protecting Students and Civil Rights in the Educational Environment
ISBN: 978-1-60787-173-6

Project Manager:	Sharon Wynne, MS
Project Coordinator:	Justin Dooley, Esq.
Content Coordinators/Authors:	Justin Dooley, Esq.
	Nina Lewis, Esq.
	Rebecca Sanin, Esq., MA
Sample test:	Rebecca Sanin, Esq., MA
Editors: Managing	Justin Dooley, Esq.
Proof readers:	Connie Day
Copy editor:	Connie Day
Pre-Flight:	Kesel Wilson
Production:	Kesel Wilson

ORELA CIVIL RIGHTS

Table of Contents

Study Tips

1. **<u>You are what you eat.</u>** Certain foods aid the learning process by releasing natural memory enhancers called CCKs (cholecystokinin) composed of tryptophan, choline, and phenylalanine. All of these chemicals enhance the neurotransmitters associated with memory and certain foods release memory enhancing chemicals. A light meal or snacks from the following foods fall into this category:

   - Milk
   - Nuts and seeds
   - Rice
   - Oats
   - Eggs
   - Turkey
   - Fish

The better the connections, the more you comprehend!

2. **<u>The pen is mightier than the sword</u>.** Learn to take great notes. A by-product of our modern culture is that we have grown accustomed to getting our information in short doses. We've subconsciously trained ourselves to assimilate information into neat little packages. Messy notes fragment the flow of information. Your notes can be much clearer with proper formatting. ***The Cornell Method*** is one such format. This method was popularized in *How to Study in College,* Ninth Edition, by Walter Pauk. You can benefit from the method without purchasing an additional book by simply looking the method up online.

3. Below is a sample of how *The Cornell Method* can be adapted for use with this guide.

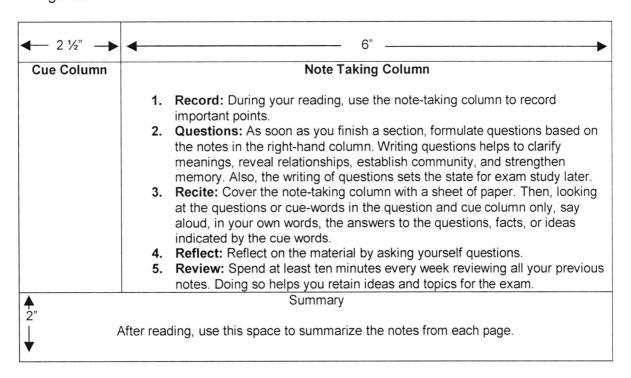

← 2 ½" →	← —————————————— 6" —————————————— →
Cue Column	**Note Taking Column**
	1. **Record:** During your reading, use the note-taking column to record important points.
	2. **Questions:** As soon as you finish a section, formulate questions based on the notes in the right-hand column. Writing questions helps to clarify meanings, reveal relationships, establish community, and strengthen memory. Also, the writing of questions sets the state for exam study later.
	3. **Recite:** Cover the note-taking column with a sheet of paper. Then, looking at the questions or cue-words in the question and cue column only, say aloud, in your own words, the answers to the questions, facts, or ideas indicated by the cue words.
	4. **Reflect:** Reflect on the material by asking yourself questions.
	5. **Review:** Spend at least ten minutes every week reviewing all your previous notes. Doing so helps you retain ideas and topics for the exam.
↑ 2" ↓	**Summary** After reading, use this space to summarize the notes from each page.

*Adapted from *How to Study in College,* Ninth Edition, by Walter Pauk, ©2008 Wadsworth

4. **See the forest for the trees.** In other words, get the concept before you look at the details. One way to do this is to take notes as you read, paraphrasing or summarizing in your own words. Putting the concept in terms that are comfortable and familiar may increase retention.

5. **Question authority.** Ask why, why, why. Pull apart written material paragraph by paragraph and don't forget the captions under the illustrations. For example, if a heading reads *Stream Erosion* put it in the form of a question (why do streams erode? Or what is stream erosion?) then find the answer within the material. If you train your mind to think in this manner you will learn more and prepare yourself for answering test questions.

6. **Play mind games.** Using your brain for reading or puzzles keeps it flexible. Even with a limited amount of time your brain can take in data (much like a computer) and store it for later use. In ten minutes you can: read two paragraphs (at least), quiz yourself with flash cards, or review notes. Even if you don't fully understand something on the first pass, your mind stores it for recall, which is why frequent reading or review increases chances of retention and comprehension.

7. **<u>Place yourself in exile and set the mood.</u>** Set aside a particular place and time to study that best suits your personal needs and biorhythms. If you're a night person, burn the midnight oil. If you're a morning person set yourself up with some coffee and get to it. Make your study time and place as free from distraction as possible and surround yourself with what you need, be it silence or music. Studies have shown that music can aid in concentration, absorption, and retrieval of information. Not all music, though. Classical music is said to work best.

8. **<u>Get pointed in the right direction.</u>** Use arrows to point to important passages or pieces of information. It's easier to read than a page full of yellow highlights. Highlighting can be used sparingly, but add an arrow to the margin to call attention to it.

9. **<u>Check your budget.</u>** You should at least review all the content material before your test, but allocate the most amount of time to the areas that need the most refreshing. It sounds obvious, but it's easy to forget. You can use the study rubric above to balance your study budget.

> The proctor will write the start time where it can be seen and then, later, provide the time remaining, typically 15 minutes before the end of the test.

Testing Tips

1. **Get smart, play dumb.** Sometimes a question is just a question. No one is out to trick you, so don't assume that the test writer is looking for something other than what was asked. Stick to the question as written and don't overanalyze.

2. **Do a double take.** Read test questions and answer choices at least twice because it's easy to miss something, to transpose a word or some letters. If you have no idea what the correct answer is, skip it and come back later if there's time. If you're still clueless, it's okay to guess. Remember, you're scored on the number of questions you answer correctly and you're not penalized for wrong answers. The worst case scenario is that you miss a point from a good guess.

3. **Turn it on its ear.** The syntax of a question can often provide a clue, so make things interesting and turn the question into a statement to see if it changes the meaning or relates better (or worse) to the answer choices.

4. **Get out your magnifying glass.** Look for hidden clues in the questions because it's difficult to write a multiple-choice question without giving away part of the answer in the options presented. In most questions you can readily eliminate one or two potential answers, increasing your chances of answering correctly to 50/50, which will help out if you've skipped a question and gone back to it (see tip #2).

5. **Call it intuition.** Often your first instinct is correct. If you've been studying the content you've likely absorbed something and have subconsciously retained the knowledge. On questions you're not sure about trust your instincts because a first impression is usually correct.

6. **Graffiti.** Sometimes it's a good idea to mark your answers directly on the test booklet and go back to fill in the optical scan sheet later. You don't get extra points for perfectly blackened ovals. If you choose to manage your test this way, be sure not to mismark your answers when you transcribe to the scan sheet.

7. **Become a clock-watcher.** You have a set amount of time to answer the questions. Don't get bogged down laboring over a question you're not sure about when there are ten others you could answer more readily. If you choose to follow the advice of tip #6, be sure you leave time near the end to go back and fill in the scan sheet.

Do the Drill

No matter how prepared you feel it's sometimes a good idea to apply Murphy's Law. So the following tips might seem silly, mundane, or obvious, but we're including them anyway.

1. Remember, you are what you eat, so bring a snack. Choose from the list of energizing foods that appear earlier in the introduction.
2. You're not too sexy for your test. Wear comfortable clothes. You'll be distracted if your belt is too tight, or if you're too cold or too hot.
3. Lie to yourself. Even if you think you're a prompt person, pretend you're not and leave plenty of time to get to the testing center. Map it out ahead of time and do a dry run if you have to. There's no need to add road rage to your list of anxieties.
4. Bring **sharp, number 2 pencils.** It may seem impossible to forget this need from your school days, but you might. And make sure the erasers are intact, too.
5. No ticket, no test. Bring your admission ticket as well as **two** forms of identification, including one with a picture and signature. You will not be admitted to the test without these things.
6. You can't take it with you. Leave any study aids, dictionaries, notebooks, computers and the like at home. Certain tests **do** allow a scientific or four-function calculator, so check ahead of time if your test does.
7. Prepare for the desert. Any time spent on a bathroom break **cannot** be made up later, so use your judgment on the amount you eat or drink.
8. Quiet, Please! Keeping your own time is a good idea, but not with a timepiece that has a loud ticker. If you use a watch, take it off and place it nearby but not so that it distracts you. And **silence your cell phone.**

To the best of our ability, we have compiled the content you need to know in this book and in the accompanying online resources. The rest is up to you. You can use the study and testing tips or you can follow your own methods. Either way, you can be confident that there aren't any missing pieces of information and there shouldn't be any surprises in the content on the test.

If you have questions about test fees, registration, electronic testing, or other content verification issues please visit www.orela.nesinc.com.

Good luck!

Sharon Wynne
Founder, XAMonline

SUBAREA 1   **LEGAL FOUNDATIONS**

COMPETENCY 0001   **UNDERSTAND FEDERAL AND STATE LAWS THAT PROTECT INDIVIDUAL CIVIL RIGHTS AND PROHIBIT DISCRIMINATION IN EDUCATIONAL SETTINGS, AS WELL AS ETHICAL STANDARDS FOR EDUCATORS IN OREGON**

Skill 1.1   **Recognizing categories of discrimination in educational settings addressed by federal and state laws and regulations (*e.g., race, national origin, religion, sex, age, disability, marital status*)**

The due process clause of the Constitution of the United Sates indicates that no state can deprive any person of life, liberty, or property without due process of law. Liberty and property have been broadly defined to refer to a wide range of substantive rights. For example, educators' contracts provide them with a property interest and expectation of employment for the term of the contract. Tenure provides an expectation of future employment and so endows the individual who has tenure with a property interest.

Liberty interest has been defined to encompass a wide range of personal freedoms. The courts have described liberty as consisting of fundamental rights that are "essential to the orderly pursuit of happiness by free men." The due process clause declares that no state can deprive a citizen of the United States of a substantive right without according that citizen due process of the law.

This clause has major implications for educators for several reasons. It makes the earlier amendments applicable to the states. Prior to the Fourteenth Amendment, the earlier amendments applied to the federal government only. Another important factor lies in the nature of public education: It is a state governmental function. When educators are acting in their professional capacities, they are "the state." Therefore, when administrators interact with teachers and students, they must be sure that they are functioning in a way that does not deprive any individual of his or her substantive rights.

In addition to the substantive interests cited above, the freedoms identified in the earlier amendments are considered substantive. For example, if a teacher is fired from his or her position for speaking out on an issue of public interest in the middle of the school year, the teacher can bring legal action in the federal courts because the state (the school system) deprived him or her of free speech rights. The teacher would also have to be accorded procedural due process because of the property interest in the remainder of the annual contract. In another example, before a student can be suspended for a significant period of time, that student must be accorded procedural due process, because the right to an education accrues to the student as a property interest through the state constitution. The sources of substantive rights are multiple and varied, but regardless of the source, the due process clause of the Fourteenth

Amendment will protect them. The major elements of procedural due process are notice, a hearing, and an impartial tribunal.

Types of Discrimination: Protected Classes

The Fourteenth Amendment includes the equal protection clause, which guarantees that laws will provide equal treatment and will be nondiscriminatory. The Fourteenth Amendment required the federal government and states to pass legislation that would implement equal protection. The most important of these federal laws for educators are discussed in Skill 1.2

There are groups of people that antidiscrimination laws specifically protect. Federal law protects people from discrimination on the basis of race, color, national origin, religion, gender, age, and disability. Oregon law protects all of the federal classes and also protects people from discrimination on the basis of sexual orientation and gender identity. This means that it is illegal for a federal or state organization to discriminate against a person on the basis of race, color, national origin, religion, gender, age, and/or disability. Similarly, the state of Oregon and its organizations and employees cannot discriminate against anyone on the basis of race, color, national origin, religion, gender, sexual orientation, and/or gender identity.

Teachers and administrators are employed by public schools, which are paid for in large part by taxes. Public schools involve compulsory requirements for student attendance, standards and state certifications for teachers, and testing and assessment requirements of the state. Thus the teachers and administrators employed by public schools are state actors, meaning they are acting on behalf of a governmental body and must ensure that students' rights are not violated. Unlike private business owners, who can deny membership in and access to their business for a myriad of reasons, teachers and administrators have the responsibility of protecting students' constitutional rights.

Race, Color, and National Origin The term "race" is used to describe the categorization of people into various groups based on heritable characteristics. Some students identify as being of one race, and others identify as belonging to multiple racial groups. Race is a social construct that has changed over time in response to cultural and political influences. Educators must not show favoritism toward any specific group of students, nor may they demonstrate indifference toward any students on the basis of race, color, or national origin. Such actions are illegal.

Religion Schools must make accommodations to address the religious needs of students. There are many ways in which schools can both accommodate students' religious needs and also create policies that are regularly reviewed to ensure that as new religions and belief systems emerge, students' beliefs and values are not being hindered. For example, a student who is absent for a religious holiday or reason should be excused and should have a reasonable time to make up the work missed. Dress code polices must be reviewed to ensure that they do not have a discriminatory effect. For example, even if school policy forbids the wearing of baseball caps and hats, it mustn't disallow the wearing of turbans or other religious garments. Schools also must ensure that they are not ignoring bullying based on religious clothing or practice and that they set, in policy and practice, a tone that accommodates students' religious beliefs.

Sex, Marital Status, and Sexual Orientation Gender and marital status are protected classes throughout the United States. Favoritism or gender-biased policy making in schools is prohibited. Similarly, educators should avoid favoring students of a particular gender. In Oregon, sexual orientation is also a protected class, and schools must not discriminate against students on the basis of their sexual preference or gender identity. This includes students who are transgender (that is, students who are physically one gender but associate strongly with the other gender).

Disability There are multiple definitions of disability, depending on the law that is being applied. The broad definition of disability under the Americans with Disabilities Act (ADA) is any mental or physical impairment that significantly limits major life activity. Someone whom others perceive as having such an impairment is also defined as having a disability. The Individuals with Disabilities Education Act (IDEA) specifically lists disability conditions that fall under the law. These categories are:

- Autism
- Deaf-blindness
- Emotional disturbance
- Hearing impairment
- Mental retardation
- Multiple disabilities
- Orthopedic impairment
- Other health impairment
- Specific learning disability
- Speech or language impairment
- Traumatic brain injury
- Visual impairment

Age Age is a protected class in terms of government employment. As long as a person is 18 years of age or older, he or she is eligible for employment in state or federal government. The government cannot discriminate, on the basis of age in hiring, retaining, or compensating employees.

Skill 1.2 **Demonstrating knowledge of federal and state laws and regulations that protect individual civil rights, prohibit discrimination, and promote educational equity (*e.g., Title VI of the Civil Rights Act of 1964, Title III of the No Child Left Behind Act of 2001, Title IX of the Education Amendments of 1972, Americans with Disabilities Act, Oregon statutes prohibiting discrimination in employment in public schools*)**

The **Individuals with Disabilities Education Act** (IDEA) was originally enacted by Congress in 1975 to make sure that, like other children, children with disabilities had the opportunity to receive a free appropriate public education. The most recent amendments were passed by Congress in December 2004, with final regulations published in August 2006. In some senses, the law is very new, even though it has a long, detailed, and powerful history. IDEA guides how states and school districts provide special education and related services to more than six million eligible children with disabilities.

The **Family Educational Rights and Privacy Act** (FERPA) (20 U.S.C. § 1232g; 34 CFR Part 99) is a federal law that protects the privacy of student education records. The law applies to all schools that receive funds under an applicable program of the U.S. Department of Education. FERPA gives parents certain rights with respect to their children's education records. These rights transfer to the student when she or he reaches the age of 18 or attends a school beyond the high school level. Students to whom these rights have transferred are "eligible students."

Title IX of the Educational Amendments of 1972 states that no individual shall, on the basis of sex, be excluded from participation in, be denied the benefits of, or be subjected to discrimination under any educational program or activity that receives or benefits from federal assistance. This statute covers the areas of admission, educational programs and activities, access to course offerings, counseling, the use of appraisal and counseling materials, and athletics. See *Marshall v. Kirkland.*

Title VI of the Civil Rights Act of 1964 extends protection from discrimination on the basis of race, color, or national origin to any program or activity receiving federal financial assistance.

Title VII of the Civil Rights Act of 1964 states that it is unlawful for an employer to discriminate against any individual with respect to compensation, terms, conditions, or privileges of employment because of that individual's race, color, religion, sex, or national origin. Some exceptions are noted in this statute. It does not apply to a religious organization that seeks individuals of a particular religion to perform the work of the organization. Where suspect classifications (those classifications having no basis in rationality) represent bona fide occupational qualifications, they are permitted. Classifications based on merit and seniority are also acceptable under this statute. See *Ansonia BOE v. Philbrook.*

Title III of No Child Left Behind (NCLB) mandates the provision of funding and support to help school districts meet the needs of students with limited proficiency in the English language and promotes best practices in doing so. Because children without English language skills cannot demonstrate proficiency on assessments designed for students whose first language is English, it is critical to ensure that language support is provided and that the school fosters an atmosphere that does not discriminate against any students on the basis of language skills or accent. Title III created the Office of English Language Acquisition (OELA) to oversee the budget and use it to "close the achievement gap between limited English proficiency students and their native-English speaking counterparts."

Oregon Statutes Prohibiting Discrimination
In general, Oregon's state laws (statutes) mirror federal laws dealing with discrimination. This section covers the relevant Oregon statutes that educators should be aware of.

Employment Discrimination ORS 659.010-659.030 Oregon law prohibits discrimination in employment on the basis of race, gender, national origin, religion, juvenile criminal record, and age (if 18 years or above). According to these laws, it is illegal for an employer to distinguish between employees on the basis of their membership in a protected class. Thus employers cannot terminate employment, fail to hire, or provide different wages or benefits packages on the basis of these classes. For example, if they are doing the same job, an employer cannot pay a female worker less than a male worker solely on the basis of gender. However, an employer can pay those workers different wages for other reasons, such as duration of employment, according to a set pay schedule.

Disability ORS 659.400-659.460 This statute prohibits employment discrimination based on physical or mental ability. It is illegal to discriminate against an employee or candidate for hire because of disability. As long as an employee can perform the substantial duties of his or her job adequately, then the employer must make reasonable accommodations for the employee. Examples include providing a chair for someone who cannot stand for long periods of time, even though other employees in the same position are required to stand; accommodations in scheduling; food policy accommodations to allow people with certain health-related needs to eat at varying times and places throughout the day; desk placement accommodations to ensure access to bathrooms and exits; and other accommodations that reasonably accommodate employees' needs in the workplace.

Work Injuries ORS 659.410-659.470 This statute prohibits employers from discriminating against employees who are injured in the course of their work. Workers who file claims for worker's compensation cannot be discriminated against or retaliated against and must be reinstated when they are able to return to work.

Housing ORS 659.425 It is illegal to discriminate, in selling or renting a house, on the basis of race, color, gender, marital status, source of income, familial status, religion, national origin, or disability.

Public Accommodation ORS 659.037, 659.425 Places of public accommodation may not discriminate on the basis of race, religion, sex, marital status, source of income, color, national origin, age (if 18 or over), or disability.

Education ORS 659.150-659.160 This set of statutes prohibits all types of discrimination in all public schools in Oregon, including universities. It prohibits public schools, and educators in such schools, from discriminating against any person. The statute defines discrimination as "any act that unreasonably differentiates treatment, intended or unintended, or any act that is fair in form but discriminatory in operation, either of which is based on age, disability, national origin, race, marital status, religion or sex."

If a school subject to this statute is found to have engaged in discrimination, the school is subject to loss of funding and/or other sanctions until it comes into compliance. Furthermore, the school could be sued by those individuals whose rights were infringed on.

Complaints to Department of Education OAR 580-01-010 The Department of Education must investigate any complaints alleging violations of civil rights. If such an investigation leads to a finding that a school's policies or practices are discriminatory, the school must take appropriate action to come into compliance with the laws. If the school fails to do so, it could lose its funding.

Skill 1.3 **Recognizing the constitutional foundations (*e.g., First and Fourteenth Amendments to the U.S. Constitution; Article I, Bill of Rights, of the Oregon Constitution*) and legal principles (*e.g., equal treatment under the law*) underlying federal and state laws related to civil rights and discrimination**

First Amendment "Congress shall make no law respecting an establishment of religion, or prohibiting the free exercise thereof; or abridging the freedom of speech, or of the press; or the right of the people peaceably to assemble, and to petition the Government for a redress of grievances."

Religion: Establishment The establishment clause is the part of the Constitution that creates "separation of church and state." It prohibits the government from establishing a national religion or advancing any particular religion. The government is permitted to pass legislation that concerns religion or religious organizations, but the purpose of the legislation must be secular. The effect of the legislation must not either advance or inhibit religion.

Religion: Free Exercise The free exercise clause also concerns religion. Whereas the establishment clause focuses on the government's endorsement of religion, the free exercise clause deals with the effects of government actions on the religious beliefs and practices of individuals. According to the Supreme Court, there are three parts to the free exercise clause: (1) No law can be enacted that forces people to accept a particular religion. (2) All people are free to choose their own religion and practice it without interference from the state. (3) However, the government can hold criminally liable an individual whose practicing of religion thwarts a more compelling societal interest. For example, a person cannot commit murder and escape charges on the basis of freedom of religion, claiming that his or her religion requires human sacrifice.

Freedom of Speech Freedom of speech is the right of individuals to speak their opinion without censorship and to express ideas and thoughts without the threat of government reprisal. Most speech is protected by the First Amendment. However, there are specific types of speech that the Supreme Court says are not protected. Unprotected speech includes speech that incites illegal acts/subversive speech, fighting words, obscenity and pornography, commercial speech, and symbolic expression.

Freedom of the Press Freedom of the press is very similar to freedom of speech, except that it particularly protects print and electronic media. This allows the press to print or electronically publish freely, without the threat of government censorship. The only limitation on freedom of the press is that the publication and/or writer of false statements can be held liable for defamation. Thus, if a newspaper publishes false information about a person, that person can sue for damages. However, the person claiming damages will have to have "clear and convincing" evidence that the information was false *and* that it was published with "actual malice." Actual malice would be demonstrated, for example, if the writer knew that the information was untrue and published it regardless. This high standard of proof in defamation lawsuits helps maintain freedom of the press, while balancing it with the rights of individuals. See *New York Times v. Sullivan.*

Freedom of Assembly The right to assemble means that people can gather together peacefully for legal purposes. The government can prohibit people from associating in groups that promote illegal activities, such as might occur in gang membership. Furthermore, the right to assemble prohibits the government from forcing groups to disclose the names of members and from discriminating against individuals on the basis of their current or past membership in a group.

Fourteenth Amendment "All persons born or naturalized in the United States, and subject to the jurisdiction thereof, are citizens of the United States and of the State wherein they reside. No State shall make or enforce any law which shall abridge the privileges or immunities of citizens of the United States; nor shall any State deprive any person of life, liberty, or property, without due process of law; nor deny to any person within its jurisdiction the equal protection of the laws."

Incorporation Doctrine The rights guaranteed to U.S. citizens by the federal government in the Bill of Rights are here extended to state governments as well. For example, any state law that hampers free speech can and should be overturned because it violates the First Amendment via the Fourteenth Amendment. The lawsuit would be based on the Fourteenth Amendment because the First Amendment applies to the federal government, not to state governments.

The important legal principles inherent in the Fourteenth Amendment are privileges and immunities, equal protection, and due process.

Privileges and Immunities This principle protects U.S. citizens from unreasonable state action.

Equal Protection The equal protection principle guarantees that all people in the United States (citizens and non-citizens) are equally protected by laws. This clause was utilized to declare segregation unconstitutional and to support affirmative action. It is the foundation of all laws concerning inequality and discrimination and is extremely important for U.S. civil rights legislation.

Due Process The due process clause incorporates the most important rights enumerated in the Bill of Rights. This means that states cannot deny their residents most of the freedoms guaranteed by the Bill of Rights, such as freedom of speech, freedom of religion, and the like. This incorporation is selective, however, and does not include the right to bear arms (Amendment II), the right against being forced to quarter soldiers (Amendment III), or the right to be indicted by a grand jury (Amendment V). Due process requires that a state's constitution provide the same protections for citizens as the U.S. Constitution. This is a minimum standard. Thus state constitutions can provide more protections than the U.S. Constitution, but not less. Oregon's state constitution provides more than the minimum.

The Supreme Court uses two different standards to determine whether a law violates due process. Laws about economic affairs, employment, and other business topics will be struck down only if there is no "rational government purpose" for the law. By contrast, laws concerning fundamental freedoms and rights will be invalidated unless the law serves a serious government purpose.

All people within the jurisdiction of a particular state have equal protection. Due process and equal protection are used in cases where distinctions are made between citizens of different states. For example, a state university is allowed to charge students different tuition fees on the basis of their state of residence (in state or out of state) if the practice advances legitimate state interests.

Article I, Bill of Rights, Oregon State Constitution

"**Section 1. Natural Rights Inherent in People** We declare that all men, when they form a social compact are equal in right: that all power is inherent in the people, and all free governments are founded on their authority, and instituted for their peace, safety, and happiness; and they have at all times a right to alter, reform, or abolish the government in such manner as they may think proper." (Equal Rights)

"**Section 2. Freedom of Worship** All men shall be secure in the Natural right, to worship Almighty God according to the dictates of their own consciences." (Freedom of Religion)

These and the other relevant sections (enumerated below) in the Bill of Rights, Oregon State Constitution, address the following:

1. Natural rights inherent in people
2. Freedom of worship
3. Freedom of religious opinion
4. No religious qualification for office
5. No money to be appropriated for religion
6. No religious test for witnesses or jurors

7. Freedom of speech and press

8. Equality of privileges and immunities of citizens

9. Assemblages of people; instruction of representatives; application to legislature

10. Emigration

11. Taxes and duties; uniformity of taxation

12. Enumeration of rights not exclusive

Skill 1.4   Applying knowledge of standards and guidelines for acting fairly, ethically, and with integrity in varied educational contexts, as outlined in the Standards for Competent and Ethical Performance of Oregon Educators

When students misbehave in school or break the school rules, administrators must follow due process. The first course of action is to interview the student and try to determine the reasons for the behavior. If the behavior is minor in nature, the principal may decide to give the student after-school detention with parental notification.

In-school suspensions are also quite common. Under this method the student is not permitted to have contact with his or her peers during the day, or during part of the day in certain cases. If the misbehavior is of a major nature, the student is likely to receive an in-school suspension for the first offense. The parents and the school board should be notified in writing. Schools have their own rules for how many in-school suspensions must occur before the student is suspended from school for a specified period of time.

The type of punishment handed out to students also depends on the age and grade level. For middle school and high school students, suspensions of up to 15 days are possible after the second or third violation. In high schools, some student actions may actually be illegal, so a law enforcement agency has to be involved. Any parent who does not agree with the suspension or punishment meted out has the right to grieve the situation. This is done by meeting with the administration and the teachers involved. If this meeting does not resolve the situation, then a further meeting may be required with the superintendent.

Oregon educators must be aware of the laws described in these materials and are required by law to be diligent in obeying them. This means that educators must be aware of their own behavior in the setting. Educators must not violate the civil rights of their students, of coworkers, or of the public. If an educator is found to have violated these provisions, the school district could be liable for damages, and the teacher may be held personally liable in a civil lawsuit. Teachers are role models and public servants. They must uphold the ideals of the Constitution and set a positive example for students and the public.

Many forms of illegal discrimination are blatantly obvious, but educators also need to be aware of subtler forms of illegal discrimination that can occur in a classroom. For example, using racial slurs and derogatory language to refer to students is clearly discriminatory. However, there are other forms of discrimination that are less noticeable to a casual observer but are equally prohibited under the law. Two forms of this subtle discrimination are the "invisible student" and the "very visible student."

The Invisible Student The invisible student is a phenomenon that occurs when an educator fails to recognize or pay attention to students of a particular race, gender, or the like. Ignoring a group of students constitutes unequal treatment and is discriminatory. Not calling on students of a particular group or barring them from participation in class discussion is discriminatory. Even if an educator has good intentions or believes she or he is shielding the student(s) from ridicule by classmates, this unequal treatment is discriminatory. "Invisible student" discrimination often happens when students are not native English speakers and teachers find them difficult to understand. By ignoring these students, educators send a message to the general student body that particular students are not worthy of consideration.

The Very Visible Student When a teacher praises or compliments a student on the basis of his or her race, national origin, gender, or the like, the teacher is drawing attention to that student that could lead other students to stereotype students of a particular protected class. For example, say a teacher is passing back math tests to her class and remarks, "As always, Ronnie and Kim got 100 percent!" referring to the only students of Asian origin in her class. This makes these students particularly visible to the other students and could lead to stereotyping of Asian students as superior in math to students of other ethnicities. The educator has singled out students and differentiated expectations for them on the basis of their ethnic group. Similarly, when a teacher praises female students for keeping the classroom tidy and praises male students for academic excellence, students may begin to feel that women are not able to achieve high academic scores and that male students should not help with classroom cleaning duties. Making students of a particular protected class visible for certain behaviors or tasks is a form of illegal discrimination.

Educators are expected to be ethical, professional, and responsible. It is strictly forbidden for educators to engage in any sort of sexual harassment of students or coworkers. If an educator believes that a student is romantically interested in him or her, the educator must report this to a supervisor immediately. For example, if a student makes advances toward an educator, the educator is required to report it.

http://policy.osba.org/albany/G/GCAA%20D1.PDF

Skill 1.5 **Identifying procedures available to teachers and students for seeking recourse when laws relating to civil rights, civil liberties, or discrimination may have been violated, and recognizing educators' personal responsibility for reporting and responding to violations of federal and state antidiscrimination laws**

Educators
Teacher Standards and Practice Commission
Complaint form available online.

1. The Office of Civil Rights

    a. Title IX of the Education Amendments of 1972

    b. Title VI of the Civil Rights Act of 1964

    c. Section 504 of the Rehabilitation Act of 1973

    d. The Americans with Disabilities Act (ADA)

2. The school district

    a. Title IX

    b. Section 504

    c. ADA

3. The Oregon Department of Education

    a. The Individuals with Disabilities Education Act (IDEA)

    b. Section 504

4. Teacher Standards and Practice Commission

COMPETENCY 0002 **UNDERSTAND FEDERAL AND STATE COURT DECISIONS RELATED TO INDIVIDUAL CIVIL RIGHTS AND DISCRIMINATION IN EDUCATIONAL SETTINGS**

Skill 2.1 **Examining federal and state court decisions that address individual civil rights including freedom of speech, freedom of the press, and freedom of religion (*e.g., Tinker v. Des Moines Independent Community School District, Hazelwood School District v. Kuhlmeier, Harper v. Poway Unified School District*)**

See also Skill 2.2

Tinker v. Des Moines: **Freedom of Speech**
The Tinkers were students in Des Moines during the Vietnam War era. Their school district passed a regulation that forbade students to protest the war at school. The Tinkers and a few other students wore armbands to school to show their opposition to the war. Teachers and school administrators asked the students to remove the armbands. The students refused to do so and were suspended from school. They felt that the armbands were a way of speaking out and that the school was violating their First Amendment right to freedom of speech. The case went all the way to the U.S. Supreme Court. The Court agreed with the students. The Court said that students are people and have rights under the Constitution, even while at school. The only conditions under which a teacher, administrator, or school district can legally infringe on those rights is when they can show that the student behavior seriously interferes with "the requirements of appropriate discipline in the operation of the school."

Hazelwood v. Kuhlmeier: **Freedom of Speech**
Students in the journalism class at Hazelwood High School wrote and edited a school newspaper that was distributed to students and teachers at the school. When the students had finished their edition of the paper and were ready to print it, they sent a draft to the principal for approval. There were some articles in the paper that the principal thought were inappropriate. For example, there was an article about sex and teenage pregnancy. It described students at the school who were pregnant, though it did not state their names. The principal was concerned that other students would be able to figure out whom these students were and that the latter might be embarrassed. He also felt that these issues were too mature for ninth-grade students. Another article he disapproved of talked about divorce. In it a student was quoted saying critical things about her father. Instead of asking the students to withdraw those articles, the principal printed the paper but removed the pages containing the articles he did not like. This meant that other, acceptable articles on those pages were withdrawn as well. Students felt this was unfair and claimed that their First Amendment rights had been violated. The U.S. Supreme Court agreed with the principal. Schools must be able to set high standards of speech for their students. Teachers and administrators do not violate students' rights by controlling the content of student speech as long as they are controlling the speech for "legitimate pedagogical concerns." This means that if teachers or administrators have a real purpose related to education and the learning

environment at the school, they are permitted to censor student speech.

Harper v. Poway: Freedom of Speech

Harper was a student at Poway High School. Harper wore a shirt that had anti-gay statements on it and a series of biblical messages condemning homosexuals. A teacher sent Harper to the principal's office. The teacher felt that the shirt distracted other students and was worried that the students might start fighting. There had been some other fistfights at Poway because of conflicting views about homosexuality. The principal asked Harper to remove or cover his shirt, and Harper refused. Because he would not change his shirt, Harper was not allowed to return to class. Harper felt he had a right to express his opinion and believed that the school was violating his First Amendment right to freedom of speech. The Court agreed with the school. The judges said that Harper's shirt injured other students and interfered with their right to learn. Homosexual students have a right not to be attacked physically and verbally while at school. This case shows that students have a limited right to freedom of speech in schools. Furthermore, educators can—and should—restrict that speech if it interferes with the rights of other students.

Skill 2.2	Examining federal and state court decisions that address discrimination on the basis of race, ethnicity, language, gender, age, religion, or disability (*e.g., Brown v. Board of Education of Topeka, Lau v. Nichols, United States v. Virginia, Childers v. Morgan County Board of Education, West Virginia State Board of Education v. Barnette, Board of Education v. Rowley*)

Brown v. Board of Education: Discrimination on the Basis of Race

Brown v. Board of Education put an end to the policy of racially segregated schools and public places throughout the United States. The case was originally brought in Topeka, when the parents of 20 African-American students unsuccessfully tried to register for enrollment in all-white schools. Topeka's school district operated eighteen elementary schools for white children but only four for African-American children. When the students were denied entry to the white schools, the NAACP filed on their behalf a lawsuit that was joined with four other, similar cases throughout America. Prior court cases had stated that as long as the schools were equal, then separation along racial lines was permissible. The U.S. Supreme Court disagreed. The Court said that "separate but equal is inherently unequal" and that racial segregation "violates the 14th Amendment to the U.S. Constitution, which guarantees all citizens equal protection of the laws."

Lau v. Nichols: National Origin (Language-based Discrimination)

Lau v. Nichols is a Fourteenth Amendment case dealing with discrimination against ESL (English as a Second Language) students in schools. The case was brought by a group of Chinese-American students who had limited English skills. They felt that the school system was not providing the support that they needed because of their limited language skills. They brought the case under the Civil Rights Act of 1964 as discrimination based on national origin. The case is important for educators for its affirmation of two main principles: (1) Language is so strongly tied to national origin that language-based discrimination can be considered illegal discrimination based on national origin, and (2) ESL students have a right to appropriate support from the school.

U.S. v. Virginia: Gender-based Discrimination

U.S. v. Virginia is a case that deals with discrimination on the basis of gender. The Virginia Military Institute was a public military college for men. A woman applied for admission, and admission was denied. She claimed that the college's male-only admission policy was discriminatory and violated her Fourteenth Amendment right to equal protection. This case made it clear that gender-based exclusion can legitimately occur only when there is a strong justification related to the objectives of the program.

Childers v. Morgan: Age-based Discrimination

This case challenged a school district policy of forced retirement for bus drivers at the age of 65. Drivers claimed that this policy constituted age discrimination and was illegal under the Age Discrimination in Employment Act of 1967 (ADEA), 29 U.S.C.A. Sec. 621 et seq. The rule established by the Court is that if there is a way to test individuals for skill competency, then forced retirement is discriminatory.

West Virginia Board of Education v. Barnette: Discrimination on the Basis of Religion

West Virginia had a requirement that all students and teachers must salute the flag. The state believed that the act of saluting the flag helped teach American values, a part of the statewide curriculum. A group of students refused to salute the flag because it violated their religious principles. The students were expelled from school and brought a lawsuit against the Board of Education. The Supreme Court decided that the refusal of some students to salute the flag did not infringe on the rights of other students to do so. The decision allows students to remain quiet and not partake in such activities if taking part would interfere with their religious beliefs. It is important for teachers to be aware that if a student wishes to refrain from an activity on the basis of her or his religious beliefs, the student has a right to do so.

Board of Education v. Rowley: **Discrimination on the Basis of Disability**

In *Board of Education v. Rowley*, a student with a hearing impairment requested that the school district provide a sign language interpreter. When the student's request was denied, the student felt that she was not receiving the "free appropriate public education" guaranteed by the Education for All Handicapped Children Act of 1975. This case defined the term "free and appropriate education" as instruction that is designed to meet the particular needs of the handicapped student and is supported by the services that would allow the student to benefit from instruction. These must be provided at the expense of the school district, must meet state standards, and must follow the student's individualized education program (IEP). Rowley was provided with a speech therapist for 3 hours per week and with a tutor for 1 hour each day. Rowley was studying at grade level and advancing from one grade to another each year. The Court said that she was receiving a free appropriate public education (FAPE) under the terms of the act, so it did not make the school district provide her with an interpreter.

Skill 2.3   Recognizing the constitutional principles on which federal and state court decisions that prohibit discrimination and promote educational equity are based (*e.g., personal liberty, due process of law, privacy, equal opportunity*)

See Skill 1.1

Skill 2.4   Analyzing educational situations involving constitutional issues related to civil rights, civil liberties, and discrimination

See Skills 3.1, 3.4, 3.6

SUBAREA 2   **EQUITY IN THE SCHOOL ENVIRONMENT**

COMPETENCY 0003   **UNDERSTAND STRATEGIES FOR ENSURING EQUITY, INCLUSION, AND CULTURAL AWARENESS IN THE EDUCATIONAL ENVIRONMENT**

Skill 3.1   Applying knowledge of how to create and sustain an equitable, nondiscriminatory learning environment for all students, including but not limited to students with diverse cultural, racial, language, socioeconomic, and religious backgrounds; students of either gender; students with different sexual orientations; and students with disabilities

The most important component in probing for student understanding is trust. Only if students trust their teacher will the communication process yield such information as the level of understanding a student has attained on any topic. If that component is in place, then creative questioning, which requires planning ahead, can sometimes reveal what the teacher needs to know. So can writing exercises that focus not on correctness but on recording of the student's thoughts on a topic. Sometimes, assuring students that only the teacher will see what is written is helpful in freeing them to reveal their own thoughts. When a new unit is introduced, including vocabulary lessons related to the unit can help students find the words they need to talk or write about the topic.

Students can be taught the skills that lead to factual recall, and beginning to teach those skills in very early grades will yield more successful students. For example, students need to know that experiencing a fact or an idea in several different ways increases their ability to recall it. It also helps them to know that experiences that involve more of the senses greatly enhance the ability to recall.

A classroom atmosphere that frowns on closed-mindedness and rewards openness to new and different approaches and ideas is powerful in shaping students' attitudes. Many of them come from homes that model narrow-minded judgmentalism and criticism of differentness, so there will be obstacles. However, the classroom can be powerful in the development of children's future attitudes and philosophies. And even though some students seem intractable, it is important to keep in mind that the experience of participating in a free and open classroom will have significant effects in the long run.

One important goal is to encourage all the children's curiosity about what is out there in the world that they don't know about. Teaching a lesson on a particular country (or even a tribe) that the children may not know exists and using various media to reveal what life is like there for children their own age is a good way to introduce the world. In such a presentation, positive aspects of the lives of those distant children should be included. Perhaps a correspondence with a village could be developed. It's good for children, some of whom may not live very high on the social scale in this country, to learn something about the rest of the world and thus to develop curiosity and an eagerness to know more.

What about an animal that they do not know about or know little about? The Animal Planet channel on television could be very useful in such a unit. The meerkat, for instance, is cute and funny and interesting, and Animal Planet has a series on that animal.

To develop a critical-thinking approach to the world, children need to know enough about valid and invalid reasoning to ask questions. Bringing into the classroom speeches or essays that include examples of both valid and invalid reasoning can be useful in helping students develop the ability to assess—and, when necessary, to question—the reasoning of others. Select published writers or televised speakers so the children can see that it is appropriate to examine and evaluate ideas that are accepted by some adults and to discuss what may be faulty in the thinking of even prominent and apparently successful communicators.

Classroom rules that uphold respect for all students, whatever their background, can have a positive effect on the thinking of children who come from bigoted families. If someone connected to the class is ill or dies, projects to reach out and express concern in some way, even if only in notes, can encourage the development of a caring and concerned approach to the plight of others. Also, taking part in such projects with relation to people they don't know, such as the victims of a hurricane, gives students the experience of caring about someone who is suffering. Making trips to nursing homes and perhaps taking cards or gifts can have a great impact on children of all ages. Elderly people are always grateful, and this touches children and shows them how much a kind gesture on their part can mean to others.

Skill 3.2   Identifying skills and strategies for promoting a sense of community in the classroom and ensuring positive, productive interactions among students with diverse characteristics, backgrounds, and needs

A classroom is a community of learning, and when students learn to respect themselves and the class members around them, learning is maximized. A positive environment, where open, discussion-oriented, and nonthreatening communication among all students can occur, is a critical factor in creating an effective learning culture. The teacher must take the lead and model appropriate actions and speech and must intervene quickly when a student makes a misstep and offends (often inadvertently) another student.

Communication issues that the teacher in a diverse classroom should be aware of include the following:

- Be sensitive to terminology and language patterns that may exclude or demean students. Regularly switch between using "he" and using "she" in speech and writing. Know and use the terms that ethnic and cultural groups currently use to identify themselves (for example, "Latinos" is generally preferred to "Hispanics").

- Be aware of body language (such as direct eye contact) that is intimidating or offensive to some cultures, and adjust accordingly.

- Monitor your own reactions to students to ensure that you make equivalent responses to males and females, as well as to students who are performing at different skill levels.

- Don't "protect" students from criticism because of their ethnicity or gender. Likewise, acknowledge and praise all meritorious work without singling out any one student. Both actions can make all students hyperaware of ethnic and gender differences and can provoke anxiety or resentment throughout the class.

- Emphasize the importance of discussing and considering different viewpoints and opinions. Demonstrate and express that you value all opinions and comments, and lead students to do the same.

Teachers should create a classroom climate that encourages extensive participation from the students. Collaborations and discussions are enhanced when students like and respect each other, and therefore, each student's learning can benefit. This is even truer when students participate fully. When everyone's thoughts and perspectives and ideas are offered, the class can consider each idea carefully in subsequent discussion. The more students participate, the more learning they gain via a more thorough examination of the topic.

To create this environment, teachers must first model how to welcome and consider all points of view. The teacher should then positively affirm and reinforce students for offering their ideas in front of the other students. Even if an idea or interpretation is somewhat off the mark, the teacher should welcome the idea enthusiastically, while perhaps offering a modification or (for factual misunderstandings) a corrected statement. The point is for students to feel confident and safe in expressing their thoughts or ideas. Only then will students be able to engage in independent discussions that consider and respect everyone's statements.

Skill 3.3   Recognizing factors that influence student perceptions and behaviors related to diversity and effective methods for promoting students' understanding and respect for racial, cultural, language, national origin, and other differences

Teachers need to be aware that much of what they say and do can be motivating and may have a positive effect on students' achievement. Studies have been conducted to determine the impact of teacher behavior on student performance. Surprisingly, a teacher's voice can really make an impression on students. Teachers' voices have several dimensions—volume, pitch, rate, and so on. A recent study on the effects of speech rate indicates that even though both boys and girls prefer to listen at the rate of about 200 words per minute, boys prefer slower rates overall than girls. This same study indicates that a slower rate of speech directly enhances processing ability and comprehension.

Other speech factors, such as communication of ideas, communication of emotion, distinctness/pronunciation, variation (as opposed to monotony of tone), and phrasing correlate with teaching criterion scores. These scores show that "good" teachers ("good" meaning teachers who positively impact and motivate students) use more variety in speech than do "less effective" teachers. A teacher's speech skills can have strong motivating elements. And a teacher's body language has an even greater effect on student achievement and on the ability to set and focus on goals. Teacher smiles provide support and give feedback about the teacher's affective state. A deadpan expression can actually be a detriment to the student's progress. Teacher frowns are perceived by students to mean displeasure, disapproval, and even anger. Studies also show that teacher posture and movement are indicators of the teacher's enthusiasm and energy, which emphatically influence student learning, attitudes, motivation, and focus on goals. Teachers have a greater effect on student motivation than any other people except parents.

Teachers can also enhance student motivation by planning and directing interactive, "hands-on" learning experiences. Research substantiates that cooperative group projects decrease student behavior problems and increase student on-task behavior. Students who are directly involved with learning activities are more motivated to complete a task to the best of their ability.

Young children believe that teachers have "eyes in the back of their head." The "with-it" teacher is truly aware of what the students are doing and sends this message to the students through his or her behavior. When a deviancy occurs in the classroom, the effective teacher knows which student(s) caused the problem and swiftly stops the behavior before the deviant conduct spreads to other students or becomes more serious.

The effective teacher demonstrates awareness of what the entire class is doing and is in control of the behavior of all students, even when the teacher is working with only a small group of children. In an attempt to prevent student misbehaviors, the teacher makes clear, concise statements about what is happening in the classroom, directing attention to content and to the students' accountability for their work, rather than focusing the class on misbehavior. It is also effective for the teacher to make positive statements about appropriate behavior that is observed.

Teachers must be careful to control the voice, both its volume and its tone. Research indicates that soft reprimands are more effective than loud reprimands in controlling disruptive behavior and that when soft reprimands are used, fewer are needed. The teacher who can attend to a task situation and an extraneous situation simultaneously without becoming exclusively immersed in either one is said to have "with-it-ness." This ability is absolutely imperative for teacher effectiveness and success. It can be difficult to address deviant behavior while sustaining academic flow, but this is a skill that teachers need to develop early in their careers and one that will become second nature, intuitive, and instinctive.

Verbal techniques, which may be effective in modifying student behavior and setting the classroom tone, include simply stating the student's name, explaining briefly and succinctly what the student is doing that is inappropriate, and indicating what the student should be doing. Verbal techniques for reinforcing behavior include both encouragement and praise delivered by the teacher. In addition, for verbal techniques to positively affect student behavior and learning, the teacher must give clear, concise directives while implying warmth toward the students.

It is also helpful for the teacher to display the classroom rules prominently. This will serve as a visual reminder of the behaviors expected of the students. In a study of classroom management procedures, it was established that the combination of conspicuously displayed rules, frequent verbal references to the rules, and appropriate consequences for inappropriate behaviors led to increased levels of on-task behavior.

The student's capacity and potential for academic success within the overall educational experience are products of her or his total environment: classroom and school system, home and family, neighborhood and community in general. All of these segments are interrelated and can be supportive, one of the other, or divisive, one against the other. As a matter of course, the teacher will become familiar with all aspects of the system that are pertinent to the students' educational experience. This would include not only process and protocols but also the availability of resources provided to meet the academic, health, and welfare needs of students. But it is incumbent on the teacher to look beyond the boundaries of the school system to identify additional resources, as well as issues and situations that will affect (directly or indirectly) a student's ability to succeed in the classroom.

Examples of Resources

- Libraries, museums, zoos, planetariums, etc.

- Clubs, societies and civic organizations, community outreach programs, and government agencies can provide a variety of materials and media, as well as possible speakers and presenters.

- Departments of social services operating within the local community can provide background and program information relevant to social issues that may be impacting individual students, and they can be a resource for classroom instruction regarding life skills, at-risk behaviors, and so on.

Initial contacts for resources outside of the school system usually come from within the system itself: from the school administration, teacher organizations, department heads, and other colleagues.

Examples of Issues/Situations

Students from Multicultural Backgrounds Curriculum objectives and instructional strategies may be inappropriate and unsuccessful when presented in a single format that relies on the student's understanding and acceptance of the values and common attributes of a specific culture that is not her or his own.

Parental/Family Influences The attitudes, resources, and encouragement available in the home environment may contribute to student success or failure. Families with higher incomes are able to provide increased opportunities for students. Students from lower-income families will need to depend on the resources available from the school system and the community.

Family members with higher levels of education often serve as models for students and have high expectations for academic success. And families with specific aspirations for children (regardless of their own educational background) often encourage students to achieve academic success and are most often active participants in the process.

A family in crisis (caused by economic difficulties, divorce, substance abuse, physical abuse, or the like) creates a negative environment that may profoundly affect all aspects of a student's life, particularly his or her ability to function academically. The situation may require professional intervention. It is often the classroom teacher who recognizes that a family is in a crisis situation and instigates an intervention by reporting this to school or civil authorities.

Regardless of the positive or negative impact on the students' education from outside sources, it is the teacher's responsibility to ensure that all students in the classroom have an equal opportunity for academic success. This begins with the teacher's statement of high expectations for every student, and it develops through the planning, delivery, and evaluation of instruction that provides for inclusion and ensures that all students have equal access to the resources necessary for successful acquisition of the academic skills being taught and measured in the classroom.

Skill 3.4   **Applying knowledge of skills and criteria for designing curricula and selecting materials for the learning environment (*e.g., texts, classroom displays*) that reflect diversity in positive ways and are representative of the diversity of the school and the broader society**

See Skill 3.1

Skill 3.5   **Identifying effective and appropriate educator responses to specific classroom problems related to equity and inclusion**

Ethics and Professionalism
The ethical conduct of educators is under intense scrutiny in today's classrooms. Teachers must observe stringent rules and regulations to maintain the highest standards of conduct and professionalism in the classroom. Current court cases have examined ethical violations of teachers engaged in improper communication with and even abuse of students, along with teachers engaged in drug violations and substance abuse in classrooms. It is imperative that the teachers educating today's young people have the highest regard for professionalism and be proper role models for students within and outside of the classroom.

The very nature of the teaching profession—the yearly cycle of doing the same thing over and over again—creates the tendency to fossilize, to cease growing, and to become complacent. The teachers who are truly successful are those who have built into their own approach to their jobs (and to their lives) safeguards against complacency. They see themselves as constant learners. They believe that learning never ends. They are careful never to teach their classes in exactly the same way they did the last time. They regularly reflect on what is happening to the students under their care and compare what happened this year to last year's outcomes.

Students with Special Needs

One of the first things a teacher learns is how to obtain resources and help for her or his students with special needs. All schools have guidelines for obtaining this assistance, especially since the implementation of the Americans with Disabilities Act. The first step in securing help is for the teacher to approach the school's administration or Exceptional Education Department for direction in obtaining special services or resources for qualifying students. Many schools have a committee designated for addressing these needs, such as a Child Study Team or Core Team. These teams are made up of both regular and special education teachers, school psychologists, guidance counselors, and administrators. The particular student's classroom teacher usually has to complete some initial paperwork and do some behavioral observations.

The teacher submits this information to the appropriate committee for discussion and consideration. The committee then recommends the next step to be taken. Subsequent steps often include a complete psychological evaluation along with certain physical examinations, such as vision and hearing screening and a complete medical examination by a doctor.

The referral of students for this process is usually relatively simple for the classroom teacher and requires little more than some initial paperwork and discussion. The services and resources to which the student gains access as a result of this process typically prove invaluable to the student with learning and/or behavioral disorders. At times, the teacher must go beyond the school system to meet the needs of some students. An awareness of special services and resources—along with an understanding of how to obtain them—is essential to all teachers and their students.

When the school system is unable to address the needs of a student, the teacher often must take the initiative and contact agencies within the community. Frequently there is no special policy for finding resources. It is simply up to the individual teacher to be creative and resourceful and to find whatever assistance the student needs. Meeting the needs of all students is a team effort that is most often spearheaded by the classroom teacher.

Family Involvement

Under IDEA, parent/guardian involvement in the development of the student's IEP (individualized education program) is required; indeed, it is absolutely essential for meeting the needs of the student with disabilities. IEPs must be tailored to meet the student's needs, and no one knows those needs better than the parent/guardian and other significant family members. Optimal conditions for the education of a student with disabilities exist when teachers, school administrators, special education professionals, and parents/guardians work together to design and execute the IEP.

Due Process
In the Individuals with Disabilities Education Act, Congress provides safeguards (including the right to sue in court) to protect students against improper actions on the part of schools. It also encourages states to develop hearing and mediation systems to resolve disputes. No students or their parents/guardians can be denied due process because of disability.

Inclusion, Mainstreaming, and Least Restrictive Environment
Inclusion, mainstreaming, and least restrictive environment are interrelated policies under IDEA, with varying degrees of statutory imperatives. Inclusion is the right of students with disabilities to be placed in the regular classroom. Least restrictive environment is the mandate that, to the greatest extent appropriate, children be educated with their peers without disabilities. Mainstreaming is a policy whereby students with disabilities are placed in the regular classroom, as long as such placement does not interfere with the individualized education program that has been prepared for each such student.

Every teacher in the system must understand the purpose and requirements associated with the development and implementation of individualized education programs (IEPs). Each public school student who receives special education and related services must have an individualized education program. Each IEP must be designed for one student only and must be a completely individualized document. The IEP creates an opportunity for teachers, parents, school administrators, related services personnel, and students (when appropriate) to work together to improve educational results for students with disabilities. The IEP is the cornerstone of a quality education for each child with a disability. To create an effective IEP, parents, teachers, other relevant school staff (as identified)—and often the student—must come together to evaluate the student's unique circumstances and the needs that must be addressed. These individuals pool their knowledge, experience, and commitment to design an education program (a workable plan) that will enable the student to be involved in, and to progress in, the general curriculum. The IEP guides the delivery of special education supports and services for the student with a disability.

Process and Requirements

- Step 1. A child is identified as possibly needing special education and related services. Each state is required to identify, locate, and evaluate all children with disabilities in the state who need special education and related services. Once each such child is identified, the consent of a parent or legal guardian is needed before the child may be evaluated. Evaluation needs to be completed within a reasonable time after consent is granted.

- <u>Step 2.</u> The child is evaluated. The evaluation must assess the child in all areas related to the child's suspected disability. The evaluation results will be used to determine whether the child is eligible for special education and related services and to make decisions about an appropriate education program for the child. If the parents/guardians disagree with the evaluation, they have the right to take their child for an independent educational evaluation (IEE). They can ask that the school system pay for this IEE.

- <u>Step 3.</u> Eligibility is determined. A group of qualified professionals and the parents/legal guardians review the child's evaluation results. Together, they decide whether the child is a "child with a disability," as defined by IDEA.

- <u>Step 4.</u> If the child is found eligible for services (in accordance with IDEA), he or she is eligible for special education and related services. Within 30 calendar days after a child is determined eligible, the IEP team must meet to write an IEP for the child.

- <u>Step 5.</u> The IEP meeting is scheduled and conducted by appropriate members of the school. School staff must notify all participants and attempt to accommodate parents/guardians and all other participants in scheduling the time and location of the meeting.

- <u>Step 6.</u> The IEP meeting is held and the IEP is written. Before the school system may provide special education and related services to the child for the first time, the parents/guardians must give consent. The child begins to receive services as soon as possible after the meeting. If the parents/legal guardians do not agree with the IEP and placement, they may discuss their concerns with other members of the IEP team and try to work out an agreement. If they still disagree, they can ask for mediation, or the school may offer mediation. They may file a complaint with the state education agency and may request a due process hearing, at which time mediation must be available.

- <u>Step 7.</u> Services are provided. The school system must ensure that the child's IEP is being carried out as it was written. Parents/guardians are given a copy of the IEP. Each of the child's teachers and service providers has access to the IEP and knows his or her specific responsibilities for carrying out the IEP. This includes the accommodations, modifications, and supports that must be provided to the child, in keeping with the IEP.

- <u>Step 8.</u> Progress is measured and reported. The child's progress toward the annual goals stated in the IEP is measured. His or her parents/guardians are regularly informed of their child's progress and of whether that progress is enough for the child to achieve the goals by the end of the year. These progress reports must be provided at least as often as parents/guardians are informed of the progress of their children without disabilities.

- Step 9. The IEP is reviewed. The child's IEP is reviewed by the IEP team at least once a year (more often if the parents/guardians or school officials ask for a review). If necessary, the IEP is revised. Parents/guardians, as team members, must be invited to attend these meetings. Parents can make suggestions for changes, can agree or disagree with the IEP goals, and can agree or disagree with the placement. If parents do not agree with the IEP or placement, they may discuss their concerns with other members of the IEP team and try to work out an agreement. There are several options, including additional testing, an independent evaluation, or a request for mediation (if available) or a due process hearing. They may also file a complaint with the state education agency.

- Step 10. The child is reevaluated at least every 3 years. This evaluation is often called a "triennial." Its purpose is to find out whether the child continues to be a "child with a disability," as defined by IDEA, and what the child's educational needs are. However, the child must be reevaluated more often if conditions warrant or if the child's parents/guardians or teachers ask for a new evaluation.

Contents of the IEP
By law, the IEP must include certain information about the child and the education program designed to meet his or her unique needs.

Current Performance The IEP must state how the child is currently performing in school (this information is known as the child's present level of educational performance). This information usually comes from the results of evaluations such as classroom tests and assignments, individual tests given to determine eligibility for services or during reevaluation, and observations made by parents, teachers, related service providers, and other school staff. The statement about "current performance" includes how the child's disability affects his or her involvement and progress in the general curriculum.

Annual Goals These are goals that the child can reasonably accomplish in a year. The goals are broken down into short-term objectives or benchmarks. Goals may be academic, social, or behavioral, may be related to physical needs, or may address other educational needs. The goals must be measurable.

Special Education and Related Services The IEP must list the special education and related services to be provided to the child or on behalf of the child. This includes supplementary aids and services that the child needs. It also includes modifications (changes) to the program or supports for school personnel—such as training or professional development—that will be provided to assist the child.

Participation with Children without Disabilities The IEP must explain the extent (if any) to which the child will not participate with children without disabilities in the regular class and in other school activities.

Participation in State- and District-wide Tests The IEP must state what modifications in the administration of these tests the child will need. If a test is not appropriate for the child, the IEP must state why the test is not appropriate and how the child will be tested instead.

Dates and Places The IEP must state when services will begin, how often they will be provided, where they will be provided, and how long they will last.

Transition Service Needs Beginning when the child is age 14 (or younger, if appropriate), the IEP must address (within the applicable parts of the IEP) the courses the student needs to take to reach his or her post-school goals. An account of the transition services the child will need must also be included in each of the child's subsequent IEPs.

Needed Transition Services Beginning when the child is age 16 (or younger, if appropriate), the IEP must state what transition services are needed to help the child prepare for leaving school.

Age of Majority Beginning at least 1 year before the child reaches the age of majority, the IEP must include a statement that the student has been told of any rights that will transfer to her or him at the age of majority (where applicable).

Measuring Progress The IEP must state how the child's progress will be measured and how parents/legal guardians will be informed of that progress.

Examples of Other Important Obligations

When You Suspect Child Abuse . . .
The child who is undergoing the abuse is the one whose needs must be served first. A suspected case that goes unreported may destroy a child's life—and his or her subsequent life as a functional adult. It is the duty of any citizen who suspects abuse and neglect to make a report, and it is especially important—and is required—for state-licensed and state-certified persons to make a report. All reports can be kept confidential if necessary, but it is best to disclose your identity in case more information is required of you. This is a personal matter that has no impact on qualifications for license or certification. Failure to make a report when abuse or neglect is suspected is punishable by revocation of certification and license, a fine, and criminal charges.

It is the right of any accused individual to have counsel and make a defense, as in any matter of law. The procedure for reporting makes clear the rights of the accused, who stands before the court innocent until proven guilty, with the right to representation, redress, and appeal, as in all matters of United States law. The state is cautious about receiving spurious reports but investigates any that seem plausible.

A teacher is obligated to report suspected abuse immediately. There is no time given as an acceptable or safe period of time to wait before reporting, so hesitation to report may be a cause for action against you. Do not wait once your suspicion is firm. All you need to have is a reasonable suspicion. You need not have actual proof; finding that is the job of the investigators.

Emotional Difficulties

Many safe and helpful interventions are available to the classroom teacher who is dealing with a student suffering from serious emotional disturbances. First and foremost, whenever overt behavior characteristics are exhibited, the teacher must maintain open communication with the parents and other professionals who are involved with the student. Students with behavior disorders need constant behavior modification, which may involve two-way communication between the home and the school on a daily basis.

The teacher must establish an environment that promotes appropriate behavior for all students, as well as respect for one another. The students may need to be informed of any special needs that their classmates have. The teacher should also initiate a behavior modification program for any student who exhibits emotional or behavioral disorders. Such behavior modification plans can be effective means of preventing deviant behavior. To be prepared to deal with any deviant behavior that does occur the teacher should have arranged for a safe and secure time-out place where the student can go for a respite and an opportunity to regain self-control.

Often when a behavior disorder is more severe, the student must be involved in a more concentrated program aimed at alleviating deviant behavior, such as psychotherapy. In such instances, the school psychologist, guidance counselor, or behavior specialist is directly involved with the student and provides counseling and therapy on a regular basis. This therapist is often involved with the student's family as well.

As a last resort, many families are turning to drug therapy. Once viewed as a radical step, administering drugs to children to balance their emotions or control their behavior has become a widely used form of therapy. Of course, only a medical doctor can prescribe such drugs. Great care must be exercised when giving medicine to children in order to change their behavior, especially because so many have undesirable side effects. It is important to know that these drugs relieve only the symptoms of behavior and do not get at the underlying causes. Parents and teachers need to be educated about the side effects of these medications.

Skill 3.6   **Demonstrating knowledge of educator responsibilities in regard to creating a safe, caring environment for all students; protecting students from all forms of harassment and other types of discriminatory treatment; and ensuring that the rights and dignity of all students are respected**

See Skill 3.2

Skill 3.7   **Demonstrating knowledge of how to communicate and collaborate positively and effectively with families and coworkers who have diverse needs, backgrounds, and perspectives**

When you find it necessary to communicate (whether by phone, letter, or in person) with a parent regarding a concern about a student, allow yourself a "cooling off" period before making contact with the parent. It is important that you remain professional and objective. Your purpose for contacting the parent is to elicit support and additional information that may have a bearing on the student's behavior or performance. Be careful not to demean the child or to appear antagonistic or confrontational. Be aware that the parent is likely to be quite uncomfortable with the bad news and will respond best if you take a cooperative, problem-solving approach to the issue. It is also a nice courtesy to notify parents of positive occurrences with their children. The teacher's communication with parents should not be limited to negative items.

The parent-teacher conference generally takes place for one or more of three purposes. First, the teacher may wish to share information with the parents concerning the performance and behavior of the child. Second, the teacher may be interested in obtaining information from the parents about the child. Such information may help answer questions or concerns that the teacher has. A third purpose may be to request parent support or involvement in specific activities or requirements. In many situations, more than one of these purposes is involved.

Advances in technology have made communication with parents even easier. Email can be a source of quick and effective communication (and it eliminates the "I lost the note" response from students). Some teachers maintain classroom websites that list a class calendar (and sometimes even test dates), project due dates, and provide other helpful information.

Research proves that the more the family is involved in a child's educational experience, the more that child will succeed academically. The problem is that teachers often assume parental involvement in education simply means that the parents show up to help at school events or participate in parental activities on campus. Teachers who subscribe to this belief devise clever strategies to increase parental involvement at school. However, children do not learn more just because their parents show up at school and assist with an activity. Furthermore, many parents work all day long and cannot assist in the school. Teachers, therefore, have to think of different ways to encourage parental and family involvement in the educational process.

Quite often, teachers have great success involving families by just informing families what is going on in the classroom. Newsletters are particularly effective at this. Parents love to know what is going on in the classroom; it makes them feel included. In newsletters, teachers can provide suggestions on how parents can help with the educational goals of the school. For example, teachers can recommend that parents read with their children for 20 minutes per day. To enhance effectiveness, teachers can also provide suggestions on what to do when their children come across difficult words or when they ask a question about content or comprehension. This gives parents practical strategies.

Parents often equate phone calls from teachers with news about misbehaviors of their children. Teachers can change that tone by calling parents with good news. Or they can send positive notes home with students. Teachers who make a practice of calling with good news are likely to have greater success when negative phone calls need to be made.

Teachers can also provide very specific suggestions to individual parents. For example, let's say a student needs additional assistance in a particular subject. The teacher can provide tips to parents to help them encourage deeper understandings of the subject outside class.

Teachers today deal with an increasingly diverse group of cultures in their classrooms. And although this is an exciting prospect for most teachers, it creates new challenges in dealing with a variety of family expectations.

First, teachers must show respect to all parents and families. They need to set a tone that reflects that their mission is to develop children into the best students—and the best people— they can be. And then they need to realize that various cultures have different views on how children should be educated.

Second, teachers have better success when they talk with parents personally about their students. Even though teachers may have many students, when they share personal observations and insights about each child, parents feel more confident that their child is "in the right hands."

Third, it is very important that teachers make it clear that they and the parents are partners in the children's education and development. Parents know their children best, and it is important to get feedback, information, and advice from them.

Finally, teachers need to be patient with difficult families, realizing that certain methods of criticism (including verbal attacks) are unacceptable. Some circumstances may require the teacher to get assistance from an administrator. This situation is very unusual, however, and most teachers find that when they try hard to be friendly and personal with parents, the parents reciprocate and assist in the educational program.

Skill 3.8   Demonstrating knowledge of how to recognize and respond to situations involving employment discrimination in the educational environment

Education is the gateway for positive developmental and life outcomes for students. When the educational environment is structured in such a way as to foster discriminatory objectives or when it tacitly discriminates against employees and students, the outcomes of children's education are undermined. When diversity is not valued in educational environments, children learn this message through school policies and practices. If discrimination is overt, children learn to discriminate and exclude members of their peer groups. Moreover, children from groups and classes that are discriminated against internalize these messages, negatively effecting the development of their self-concept and well-being. If discrimination is subtle, children learn that members of some groups and classes are valued over others, because young minds perceive the lack of any response to discrimination as an affirmative response in *favor* of discrimination. Employment discrimination fosters a discriminatory environment in school buildings. Employment discrimination includes illegal treatment of employees in matters related to hiring, firing, benefits, testing, retirement plans, disability leave, use of facilities, training opportunities, promotions, recruitment, and/or compensation.

Identifying Employment Discrimination in Schools
Employment discrimination fosters various types of discrimination, because children look to their educational environments for role models. When staff and faculty are homogeneous, children lose the opportunity to seek role models in adults who are members of various ethnic, religious, gender, and racial groups. Discrimination in hiring occurs when employer school districts illegally identify employees and job candidates on the basis of age, creed, disability, national origin, race, religion, sex, or other unlawful criteria. Examples of hiring/firing practices that are discriminatory include choosing female candidates to interview for elementary school positions because of a belief that women are more effective with young children; firing a teacher on the basis of his identifying himself as a Muslim; failing to advertise vacant positions; and hiring teachers of like experience and education on different pay scales reflecting their race, national origin, sex, or the like. Additional examples of employment discrimination include offering training and promotional opportunities to teachers on the basis of membership in a protected class (religion, race, sex, etc.) and, with illegal, discriminatory intent, firing an employee for utilizing her or his disability benefit.

Steps That Can Be Taken to Avoid Employment Discrimination

1. Employment discrimination in the workplace can occur when policies fail to provide employees with floating holidays and the ability to take time off from work for religious holidays and requirements. If employees are penalized for celebrating religious holidays that are not part of the school calendar, applicants for school-related positions will necessarily be filtered, excluding members of certain religious affiliations. Employment policies should include floating holidays and benefits that allow employees to celebrate religious holidays if these are not part of the school calendar.

2. Employment discrimination can occur in the educational environment when dress codes do not have exceptions for religious requirements. For example, a dress code that disallows the wearing of garments on the head (such as baseball caps) can impact those whose religions require wearing a yarmulke or covering the head. Such exceptions must be part of policies for employees.

3. All teachers should receive a policy handbook that provides information on how to address grievances and file complaints and that lists the various agencies where they can do so if they believe they have been a victim of discrimination.

4. Schools should publish statements about non-discriminatory hiring policies and display them in a number of visible places.

COMPETENCY 0004   **UNDERSTAND THE IMPLICATIONS OF STUDENT DIVERSITY FOR TEACHING AND LEARNING AND HOW TO INTERACT WITH ALL STUDENTS IN WAYS THAT PROMOTE THEIR SELF-CONFIDENCE AND ACHIEVEMENT OF EDUCATIONAL GOALS**

Skill 4.1   **Applying knowledge of strategies that educators can use to increase their own understanding of student diversity and its impact on teaching and learning**

Oftentimes, students absorb the culture and social environment around them without deciphering the contextual meaning of the experiences. When provided with a diversity of cultural contexts, students are able to adapt and incorporate multiple meanings from cultural cues vastly different from their own socioeconomic backgrounds. Sociocultural factors have a definitive impact on students' psychological, emotional, affective, and physiological development, along with their academic learning and future opportunities.

The educational experience for most students is a complicated experience with a multitude of interlocking meanings and inferences. If one aspect of the complexity is altered, it affects other aspects, which may influence how a student or teacher views an instructional or learning experience. With the current demographic profile of today's school communities, the complex task of understanding, interpreting, and synthesizing nuances of meaning from many diverse cultural lineages can be challenging indeed. It may even create obstacles to communication that can impede the acquisition of learning for students.

Personalized Learning Communities
Teachers must create personalized learning communities where every student is a valued member and contributor to classroom experiences. In classrooms where sociocultural attributes of the student population are incorporated into the fabric of the learning process, dynamic interrelationships are created that enhance the learning experience and the personalization of learning. When students are provided with numerous academic and social opportunities both to contribute to and to share in learning about sociocultural diversity, everyone in the classroom benefits from bonding through shared experiences and from having an expanded view of cultures that differ vastly from their own.

Researchers continue to show that personalized learning environments increase student learning, reduce dropout rates among marginalized students, and decrease unproductive student behavior that can result from constant cultural misunderstandings or miscues between students. Promoting diversity of learning and cultural competency in the classroom for students and teachers creates a world of multicultural opportunities and learning. For example, students are able to step outside their comfort zones and share the world of a homeless student or empathize with an ELL student (English language learner) who has just immigrated to the United States. Discovering that such a student is learning English for the first time and is still trying to keep up with the academic learning in an unfamiliar language allows students to grow exponentially in social understanding and cultural connectedness.

Personalized learning communities provide supportive learning environments that address the academic and emotional needs of students. As sociocultural knowledge is conveyed continuously in the interrelated experiences shared cooperatively and collaboratively in student groupings and individualized learning, the current and future benefits confirm the importance of understanding the "whole child," including her or his social and cultural context.

Intercultural Approaches to Learning
In personalized learning communities, relationships and connections among students, staff, parents, and community members promote lifelong learning for all students. School settings that celebrate diversity in the classroom, community, and curriculum enable students to maximize their academic capabilities and educational opportunities. Establishing a school climate that embraces opportunities to draw on the contributions of a multicultural student population creates positive and proactive mission and vision themes that align student and staff expectations.

The following factors enable students and staff to emphasize and integrate diversity into student learning:

- Inclusion of multicultural themes in curriculum and assessments

- Creation of a learning environment that promotes multicultural research, learning, collaboration, and social construction of knowledge and application

- Learning tasks that emphasize student cognitive, critical thinking, and problem-solving skills

- Learning tasks that personalize the cultural aspects of diversity and celebrate diversity in the subject matter and student projects

- Promotion of positive intercultural peer relationships and connections

Teachers communicate diversity in instructional practices and experiential learning activities that create curiosity in students who want to understand the interrelationship of cultural experiences. Students become self-directed in discovering the global world inside and outside the classroom. Teachers understand that when diversity becomes an integral part of the classroom environment, students become global thinkers and doers.

In the intercultural communication model, students are able to learn how different cultures engage in both verbal and nonverbal modes of communicating meaning. Students who become multilingual in understanding the stereotypes that have defined other cultures are able to create new bonding experiences that will typify a more integrated global culture. Students who understand how to communicate effectively with diverse cultural groups are able to maximize their own learning experiences by transmitting both verbal and nonverbal cues and expectations in project collaborations and in performance-based activities.

Students benefit exponentially from teachers who are able to engage all learners in intercultural approaches to the academic process and learning experience. Teaching students how to incorporate learning techniques from a cultural perspective enriches the cognitive experience because students become able to expand their cultural knowledge bases.

Skill 4.2 **Applying knowledge of the educational implications of student differences (*e.g., cultural background, home language, national origin, sexual orientation, disabilities, talented and gifted*) and how to meet the needs of all students in ways that promote learning and self-esteem**

Most class rosters consist of students from a variety of cultures. Teachers should get to know all their students so that they will be able to incorporate elements of all the cultures represented into classroom activities and planning. Also, getting to know about each student's background and cultural traditions helps to build rapport with each student, as well as further educating the teacher about the world in which he or she teaches. *See Skill 3.2 for more information about a culturally diverse classroom.*

Teachers must make every attempt to communicate daily with students who are still learning English. And they must find ways to encourage each such student's participation, whether with another student who speaks the same language or via word cards, computer programs, drawings, or other methods. Of course, the teacher must make sure that the appropriate language services begin for the student in a timely manner, as well.

Teachers must also consider students from various socioeconomic backgrounds. These students are just as likely as anyone else to work well in a classroom, but unfortunately, sometimes difficulties occur with these children when it comes to completing homework consistently. These students may need help in devising a homework system, or they may need more instruction on study habits or test-taking skills. Teachers should encourage these students as much as possible and offer positive reinforcement when they meet or exceed classroom expectations. Teachers should also watch these students carefully for signs of malnutrition, fatigue, and possibly learning disorders.

The primary responsibility of the classroom teacher is to ensure that all aspects of the educational process, and all information necessary to master specified skills, are readily accessible by all students in the classroom. In the classroom, the teacher must actively promote inclusion and devise presentations that address commonalities among heterogeneous groups. In the development of lesson plans and presentation formats, this should be evident in the concept and in the language used (whenever possible, for example, incorporate ideas and phrases that suggest "we" rather than "they").

Initially, the teacher must take the time to get to know each student as an individual and must demonstrate a sincere interest in each student. It is important to know the correct spelling and pronunciation of each student's name and to be aware of how the student prefers to be addressed. Plan time for interaction in the classroom so both the teacher and the class can become familiar with each student's interests and experiences. This will help the teacher and the students avoid making assumptions based on any individual's background or appearance.

Encourage all students to respond to each other's questions and statements in the classroom. Be prepared to respond appropriately when any issue or question regarding diversity arises during classroom discussions or activities. If necessary to promote or control discussion in the classroom, the teacher should provide the students with specific guidelines (which are age-appropriate and hence easy to understand and follow) defining the intended objectives and any restrictions. Inclusion means involving everyone in classroom discussions. The teacher should allow the students to volunteer and then should call on the more reluctant students to provide additional information or opinions. All opinions that are not derogatory in the particular case or in general are valid and should be reinforced as such by the teacher's approval.

The prescribed teaching material in a given subject area usually provides an adequate format appropriate to the grade level and the diversity of an average student population. By ensuring that any additional content or instructional aides presented in the classroom are thematically similar to the prescribed material, the teacher can usually assume that these will also be appropriate.

But the teacher is the final arbiter regarding content, format, and presentation in the classroom. Therefore, the teacher must exercise judgment when reviewing all classroom materials, lesson plans, presentations, and activities to be sure they meet established criteria. Consider the following examples of material that does not meet such criteria.

- *Offensive*: Anything that might be considered derogatory regarding any individual or group. Any comment or material that is insensitive to any nationality, religion, culture, race, family structure, or the like. Regardless of the composition of a particular classroom, negativism about any group implies tolerance of such negativism and contributes to a "them versus us" attitude.

- *Exclusive*: Anything that ignores or nullifies the needs, rights, or value of any individual or group. Anything that stratifies society, placing some group or groups above others in significance.

- *Inappropriate*: Anything below or beyond the suitable comprehension level. Material that is imprecise or otherwise inadequate for teaching mastery of specific skills within the subject matter. Anything that fails to provide for accurately measurable skill acquisition.

The teacher should actively work to broaden the students' sense of "we" even beyond the classroom and the local community—and indeed to foster a sense of all people as "we." For example, without using colloquialisms or local slang in lesson presentation, the teacher should demonstrate an understanding and acceptance of the richness and variety of the ways in which people communicate.

When planning instruction for a diverse group (and when teaching about diversity, for that matter), incorporate teaching through the use of perspective. There is always more than one way to "see" or approach a problem, an example, a process, a fact or event, or any learning situation. Varying the approach to instruction helps maintain the students' interest in the material and enables the teacher to address the diverse ways in which different individuals can best comprehend it.

The requirement that students within a diverse classroom acquire the same academic skills (at the same levels) can sometimes be achieved via instructional materials that incorporate programmed learning. Although it is not widely available for every subject at every level, a good deal of such useful material has been published. And professional teachers who are familiar with the programmed learning format have often created their own modules for student use, to be incorporated within their lesson planning.

Skill 4.3 **Demonstrating knowledge of behaviors that show sensitivity and responsiveness to students with diverse characteristics and needs in various educational settings**

Diversity in classroom makeup may not be as distinctive as race and ethnicity, gender, and so forth. Students who are physically or intellectually challenged may also add diversity within a general student population. A student population including members from varying socioeconomic situations also exhibits diversity. All students must be included in the learning process. Acceptance of this diversity by students, and any specific requirements necessary to help individual students achieve on a par with classmates, must be incorporated in lesson planning, teacher presentations, and classroom activities. For example, access to technology and media may vary greatly within the student population. In planning classroom work, homework assignments, and other projects, the teacher must take this into account. First, be knowledgeable about the resources available to the students directly, within the school, the library system, and the community. Be sure that any issues that might restrict a student's access (physical impediments, language difficulties, or expense, for example) are addressed. Second, never plan for work or assignments where students do not have equal access to information and technology. As in every aspect of education, all students must have an equal opportunity to succeed.

Enhancing Self-Concept
A positive self-concept is a very important element of a child's or adolescent's ability to learn and to be an integral member of society. If students think poorly of themselves or have sustained feelings of inferiority, they probably will not be able to optimize their potential for learning. It is therefore part of the teacher's task to ensure that each student develops a positive self-concept.

A positive self-concept does not imply feelings of perfection, superiority, or even competence/efficacy. Instead, a positive self-concept involves self-acceptance as a person, liking oneself, and having a proper respect for oneself. The teacher who encourages these traits has contributed to the development of a positive self-concept in students.

Teachers may take a number of approaches to enhancing self-concept among students. One such scheme is the process approach, which proposes a three-phase model for teaching. This model includes a sensing function, a transforming function, and an acting function. These three factors can be simplified into the words by which the model is usually known: reach, touch, and teach. The sensing, or perceptual, function incorporates information or stimuli in an intuitive manner. The transforming function conceptualizes, abstracts, evaluates, and provides meaning and value to perceived information. The acting function chooses actions from several different alternatives that are set forth overtly. The process model may be applied to almost any curricular field.

An approach that aims directly at the enhancement of self-concept is designated Invitational Education. According to proponents of this approach, teachers and their behaviors may be inviting or they may be disinviting. Inviting behaviors enhance self-concept among students, whereas disinviting behaviors diminish self-concept.

Disinviting behaviors include those that demean students, as well as those that may be chauvinistic, sexist, condescending, thoughtless, or insensitive to student feelings. Inviting behaviors are the opposite of these; they characterize teachers who act with consistency and sensitivity. Inviting teacher behaviors reflect an attitude of "doing with" rather than "doing to." Students are "invited" or "disinvited," depending on the teacher behaviors.

Invitational educators exhibit the following skills (Biehler and Snowman, 394):

1. Reaching each student (*e.g., learning names, having one-to-one contact*)

2. Listening with care (*e.g., picking up subtle cues*)

3. Being real with students (*e.g., providing only realistic praise, "coming on straight"*)

4. Being real with oneself (*e.g., honestly appraising your own feelings and disappointments*)

5. Inviting good discipline (*e.g., showing students you have respect in personal ways*)

6. Handling rejection (*e.g., not taking lack of student response in personal ways*)

7. Inviting oneself (*e.g., thinking positively about oneself*)

Promoting Cooperative Learning
Cooperative learning situations, as practiced in today's classrooms, grew out of searches conducted by several groups in the early 1970s. Cooperative learning situations can range from very formal applications such as STAD (Student Teams–Achievement Divisions) and CIRC (Cooperative Integrated Reading and Composition) to less formal groupings known variously as "group investigation," "learning together," and "discovery groups." Cooperative learning in the general sense is now firmly recognized and established as a teaching and learning technique in American schools.

Because cooperative learning techniques are so widely diffused in the schools, it is necessary to orient students in the skills by which cooperative learning groups can operate smoothly. Students who cannot interact constructively with other students will not be able to take advantage of the learning opportunities provided by the cooperative learning situations and will furthermore deprive their fellow students of the opportunity for cooperative learning.

These skills form the hierarchy of cooperation in which students first learn to work together as a group so that they may then proceed to levels at which they engage in simulated conflict situations. This cooperative setting makes it possible to entertain different points of view constructively.

Skill 4.4   Applying knowledge of how to treat all students equitably

Effective teaching and learning for students begin with teachers who can demonstrate sensitivity to diversity in teaching and relationships within school communities. Student portfolios include work that has a multicultural perspective wherein students share cultural and ethnic life experiences in their learning. Teachers are responsive to including cultural and diverse resources in their curriculum and instructional practices. Exposing students to culturally sensitive room decorations and posters that show positive and inclusive messages is one way to demonstrate inclusion of multiple cultures. Teachers should also continuously make cultural connections that are relevant and empowering for all students and should communicate the same academic and behavioral expectations to all. Cultural sensitivity is communicated beyond the classroom with parents and community members to establish and maintain relationships.

Teachers must establish a classroom climate that is culturally respectful and engaging for students. In a culturally sensitive classroom, teachers maintain equity and fairness in student interactions and curriculum implementation.

Assessments include cultural responses and perspectives that become further learning opportunities for students.

Here are some artifacts that can reflect teacher and student sensitivity to diversity:

- Student portfolios reflecting multicultural/multiethnic perspectives
- Journals of responses to field trips and to guest speakers from diverse cultural backgrounds
- Printed materials and wall displays from multicultural perspectives
- Parent/guardian letters in a variety of languages reflecting cultural diversity
- Projects that include cultural history
- Disaggregated student data reflecting cultural groups
- Classroom climate of professionalism that fosters diversity and cultural inclusion

Skill 4.5 **Demonstrating awareness of the importance of avoiding stereotyping students and of treating all students as individuals**

See Skill 3.6

Skill 4.6 **Applying knowledge of skills and strategies for working and interacting effectively with all students, including but not limited to students with diverse racial, cultural, and language backgrounds; students of both genders; students from various socioeconomic circumstances; students with disabilities; and students with different sexual orientations and diverse family arrangements**

See Skill 4.2

COMPETENCY 0005   **UNDERSTAND SITUATIONS INVOLVING EQUITABLE STUDENT ACCESS TO EDUCATIONAL COURSES, PROGRAMS, AND EXPERIENCES, AND NONDISCRIMINATORY GRADING AND ADVISING**

Skill 5.1   **Demonstrating knowledge of situations in which inequitable treatment of students leads to inequitable educational opportunities, including the overrepresentation or underrepresentation of certain categories of students in particular courses and programs, and ways educators can respond to these situations**

Inequitable treatment of students can lead to unequal opportunities, which result in student outcomes that are shaped by unjust school practices. There are many examples of ways in which inequitable treatment of children can result in the exclusion of certain groups of children from opportunities. In order to help ensure that equitable opportunities are available to all students, teachers should bear the following guidelines in mind.

Recognize ways in which requirements related to parent involvement can result in inequitable opportunities for different groups of students.

A policy requiring that a parent be involved in order for a student to participate can adversely affect children whose parents do not speak English and those whose parents have obstacles (such as illiteracy) that prevent their participating in their children's schooling. Such policies can also discriminate against children in poverty or children whose families are without resources. Policies should be reviewed to ensure that parental involvement is a goal, not a requirement for student participation in academic opportunities.

Identify referral practices that can result in the overrepresentation of students from certain groups among those classified as eligible for special education.

Inappropriate referrals to special education for one group of students or class of students can result in the overrepresentation of children from that group or class among those receiving special education services. Overrepresentation occurs when a group's percentage among those receiving special education services is larger than the group's percentage in the school population at large. Overrepresentation can adversely affect students in many ways. Children miss the opportunities available to those in the general education program, they may receive inappropriate intervention, their self-esteem may suffer from labelling, and they may have limited access to resources.

The following steps can be taken to determine practices that result in overrepresentation of a specific group in special education services.

1. **Ask questions about the special education referral process.** Are specific teachers over-referring students for special education intervention? Does your school refer students for special education more than similar schools in your community? Are the students referred for special education generally representative of one ethnic/racial group? Are the students referred for special education generally of low-income backgrounds? These questions address practices that result in overrepresentation of minority groups in special education classes.

2. **Review the process for referral.** What policies exist for the process of referrals? Are teachers required to document concerns for a period of time prior to making a referral? Are meetings held with families and school psychologists to identify non-academic challenges to learning before a referral for evaluation is made? For example, if a child is suddenly not meeting grade-level expectations, is there a non-academic explanation, such as a recent divorce, a change in family structure, or a recent death in the family? What was the timeframe for any pre-referral intervention, such as additional one-on-one teacher support? Was it in place long enough to influence student outcomes?

3. **Review school policies.** In order to avoid overrepresentation of a group in special education services, schools must ensure that the school culture, as evidenced by policies and practices, values diversity and respects cultural differences. For example, schools should respond to language differences by providing material for families in multiple languages, identifying English language learners, providing appropriate instruction, and ensuring that teachers have the professional development they need to support their work with children and families who represent diverse backgrounds. Districts should standardize methods for referral to special education, and if districts cannot determine why overrepresentation exists in special education services, they should seek outside support.

Identify practices that result in overrepresentation of some groups—and underrepresentation of other groups—in advanced coursework opportunities and extracurricular activities.

The following steps can be taken to help ensure that overrepresentation and underrepresentation of students in courses and extracurricular activities are not the result of school policies and practices.

1. In order to ensure that students aren't being encouraged to take classes on the basis of sex-typing or other stereotypes, schools should review the process by which guidance counsellors advise students to take certain courses or apply for various opportunities.

2. In order to avoid overrepresentation or underrepresentation, schools should compare the percentage enrollment of various categories of students in particular classes with their percentage of the overall school population. Imbalanced course enrollment may indicate practices that are fostering overrepresentation or underrepresentation. If a science course is offered and Caucasians account for 95% of the course enrollment and no Latino students enroll, the school should review whether this is disproportionate to the number of Latino students in the overall school population and, if so, should identify barriers to enrollment.

3. In order to avoid underrepresentation of certain groups in educational opportunities, coursework, and extracurricular activities, schools should look at the way in which coursework opportunities are advertised to the student body and parents to see whether there are opportunities to communicate more effectively about such opportunities and thereby achieve more equitable enrollment. For example, if opportunities to enroll in an extracurricular math program are advertised only to the AP (advanced placement) math class, which is made up largely of male students, then a simple change in practice—advertising the opportunity in *every* math class—would probably have an impact on enrollment.

Skill 5.2   **Identifying appropriate remedies for school personnel to use in responding to past practices that result in discrimination against certain categories of students and discourage their enrollment and participation in particular courses**

It is important for teachers to be familiar with the ways in which past allegations of discrimination have been addressed and to ensure that policies and practices are not exclusionary.

Past practices of discrimination in schools are part of the history of education in the United States prior to legal and educational reform. Such practices have contributed to the achievement gap and opportunity gap that plague educational institutions across the United States. In order to remedy past discriminatory practices, schools must take an affirmative approach to valuing diversity and must communicate this approach in their mission statement and in published statements on their school website, in school materials, and on displayed school posters. Moreover, schools should have information posted for teachers, parents, and students to explain the proper ways to file a complaint and should investigate any alleged practices of discrimination. Of equal importance, schools must have an internal review process and an antidiscrimination policy *that all employees receive* regarding zero tolerance for discriminatory practices and an indication of the disciplinary procedures that will be applied if alleged actions are substantiated.

Skill 5.3   **Applying knowledge of factors in the classroom (*e.g., grouping practices, testing and grading practices, teacher attitudes and behaviors*) and in the school (*e.g., tracking, advising*) that can lead to inequitable student access to courses, programs, and learning experiences, and ways educators can avoid or respond to these situations**

Assessment can take many forms and serve different purposes. The primary purpose of appraisal is to assist the counselor in helping students recognize their resources, utilize their strengths, and accept their limitations, whether the focus is academic, social, personal, or vocational. Increasingly, tests are used to measure student performance for reasons other than helping individual students with their educational and career goals. Nonetheless, it is the task of the counselor to help the student use all test results for self-understanding and growth.

Formal Assessment Tools
A variety of instruments are used for evaluation purposes. Formal tools with standardized scoring include tests administered by school counselors and other personnel, as well as tests administered by the school psychologist. The school psychologist might utilize intelligence tests, which assess the ability to learn, along with other psychological and aptitude tests in order to determine appropriate placement and develop individualized education programs when they are needed.

School counselors, teachers, and others may administer achievement tests (which evaluate how much has been learned), state tests measuring student performance, college entrance and preparatory tests (such as the SAT, PSAT, and ACT), advanced placement (AP) tests, and others. These tests, though administered at school, are scored offsite by the testing company that prepares and distributes the tests.

Other formal means of appraisal include inventories that measure aptitude, vocational interests, personality traits, and learning styles. Many of these are scored by the school counselor or other personnel administering the test. Counselors may also use assessment tools designed to focus on behavioral issues; examples include the incomplete sentence test, lethality inventories, suicide risk assessments, and depression inventories. These inventories must be used with caution and only by counselors with appropriate background and training.

Informal Assessment Tools
School counselors may find that they use informal means of assessment more frequently. These may involve using some of the inventories mentioned above as discussion tools rather than as formal assessments. They also include behavioral observation of the student in the classroom or other settings, feedback forms developed to evaluate specialized guidance programs, behavior surveys, and needs assessments. The value of all informal assessment tools lies in their ability to give the counselor information that can enhance his or her work with students and, in many cases, increase the student's self-awareness.

Purposes for Which Appraisal Can Be Used

1. To help students recognize and utilize the resources within themselves

2. To improve self-understanding and enhance self-concept

3. To assess the student's behavior and help the counselor and student anticipate the student's future behavior

4. To stimulate the student to consider new interests for further exploration and to develop realistic expectations

5. To provide meaningful information that can help the student make intelligent decisions

6. To aid the counselor and student in identifying and developing future options

The Limitations of Appraisal

1. The use of tests can sometimes interfere with the relationship the counselor has developed with the student, especially if the student is sensitive to being evaluated.

2. There may be a tendency to allow test results to dictate a course of action without considering many other factors. Care needs to be taken not to make assumptions about the student's abilities and choices on the basis of testing alone.

3. If the results of the test are not presented to the student in a manner that promotes self-understanding, more damage than good can result from taking the test.

4. The use of tests tends to put the counselor in the position of an authority, so the student may perceive the test results as the absolute truth, rather than as just one of many sources of useful insights.

5. Many informal assessment tools, though helpful in generating discussion, can be used too subjectively by both the counselor and the student.

Assessment for Other Purposes

Ideally, tests are administered when the student feels the need for additional information to use in making decisions about educational or career development planning. When the student decides to take a test, motivation is likely to be high, and this enhances the test's accuracy. Some tests, however, are administered because the school district or the state mandates their use. These are primarily performance and achievement tests. The stated purpose is to use student achievement levels to assess the effectiveness of the school's educational programs and to identify areas where improvement is needed.

Conditions That Affect Test Results

Testing Room Environment The comfort of the room and the desk or table and chairs can affect the outcome of the test. The room should be well lighted and ventilated, as well as free of noise and extraneous sound. A minimum distance should be maintained between desks, test takers should occupy alternating seats if possible, and the students should be able to hear the directions clearly. The desk should be large enough to provide enough writing space for both the test and the answer sheet.

Physical and Mental Condition of the Test Taker The scores obtained on any test depend to a certain extent on the student's physical and mental condition. Tests should never be scheduled to conflict with other school activities. Such other activities include, but are not limited to, exam week for termination of courses in progress, vacations, and extracurricular activities such as proms and sports events. Students tend to overestimate their physical stamina and do not take into consideration the fact that physical exhaustion adversely affects mental function. Related conditions that are beyond the control of the counselor include the stress the student is experiencing, the atmosphere at home, and social conflict with peers that may have erupted immediately before the exam.

Preparation of the Test Taker This includes both academic preparation (if an achievement test is to be administered) and the information given to the student about the mechanics of the test. Motivation to do well on the exam is also an important part of preparation.

Validity of the Test If the test does not test what it is supposed to test, there is no reason to administer the exam. It is not only a waste of the student's and the counselor's time but is also detrimental to the motivation of the student in sitting for future tests. And of course there is the added danger that incorrect and invalid results will be used to determine future goals and placements.

Skill 5.4	**Demonstrating knowledge of factors contributing to the disproportionate enrollment of students with particular racial, cultural, language, and socioeconomic backgrounds in special education programs and appropriate methods used by educators to address this problem**

See also Skill 5.1

Course Options and Scheduling
School counselors are intimately involved in helping students schedule their coursework at the middle and high school levels. Even elementary school counselors may be in a position to help students and parents/guardians make choices about academic pathways and elective courses. Course selection is an ongoing process throughout the student's years at school.

It is essential that counselors be familiar with the school's curriculum and have a good grasp of the basic schedule, as well as of prerequisites and other special requirements for certain courses. They must understand the links between various academic tracks and courses and their relationship to different career and postsecondary education options. Equally crucial is an awareness of each student's interests, abilities, and prior coursework, along with any relevant assessment data.

Each district has procedures that outline how students may sign up for courses and how parental approval is recorded. Some districts have strict policies about admission into certain classes, such as advanced placement or higher-level courses. Some schools also offer cross-education with local colleges and universities, as well as with vocational and technical schools. Counselors need to be familiar with all the options available to a wide variety of students interested in a range of careers and educational pathways.

Individualized Education Programs

A number of students will also have individualized education programs (IEPs). These may be students with cognitive impairment, learning problems, physical disabilities, social or emotional issues, or some other exceptionality. School counselors are not solely responsible for developing these plans but are part of a team that may involve the school psychologist, the school nurse, special education teachers and administrators, the school social worker, the parents/guardians, and/or outside service providers. School counselors need to be familiar with each student's IEP and must adhere to the school district's procedures regarding their role in implementing the IEP.

Skill 5.5   Demonstrating knowledge of the problems of discriminatory grading and advising based on gender, racial, and other stereotypes and ways educators can avoid these problems

Discriminatory grading and advising on the basis of gender, racial, and other stereotypes result in inequitable, unjust student outcomes based on criteria other than actual academic skill or quality of work product. Such practices can adversely affect students' access to higher education, limit their opportunities for advanced placement coursework in high school, and deprive them of future career opportunities. Such practices also have the potential to undermine students' self-confidence, self-esteem, and psychological well-being. There are several ways in which educators can prevent such practices.

Identify practices that result in discriminatory grading and advising, and gain knowledge about avoiding these practices.

1. **Review assessment measures.** Do students have multiple opportunities to demonstrate their knowledge utilizing different skills? Multiple assessments enable students who may have test anxiety or difficulty responding to testing environments to demonstrate their knowledge through essay writing and other assessments. Students with various learning disabilities may have difficulty expressing their competency with certain kinds of assessments and thus need multiple ways to demonstrate their knowledge.

2. **Review tests and assessments to ensure that they are culturally competent and don't favor a specific ethnic group or class in the classroom.** For example, if testing uses language that is more familiar to children from certain backgrounds, then children from different backgrounds will be at a disadvantage in answering questions. For example, in a district with a large impoverished population, students from one part of town may have less exposure to language, art, and culture than children from another part of town. Using test questions that include references to places and environments frequented only by some of the children in the class may also create an advantage for one group and a disadvantage for another.

3. **Employ blind grading.** Where appropriate, utilize blind grading methods by assigning students ID numbers and grading tests and assignments accordingly, so that the teacher who is grading the work does not know what student submitted it.

4. **Review guidance departments and decision-making processes for placement and course alternatives.** If guidance departments are not analyzed and reviewed, "steering practices" may arise—that is, counsellors may steer students in one direction or another on the basis of sex (medical school versus nursing), race (vocational school versus college), or other unlawful criteria.

Skill 5.6   Identifying situations in which separation of students according to sex, disability status, or other criteria is legally acceptable (*e.g., separation by sex in contact sports in physical education classes, ability grouping for some classroom activities*) and situations in which such separation is not legally acceptable

Generally, students cannot be separated on the basis of race, sex, disability, or any other characteristic that places them in a protected class. In certain situations, however, students can be separated according to various criteria in a legally permissible manner. For example, students are often separated by sex for contact sports in which failure to separate children could result in injury or inappropriate contact. In order for students to be lawfully separated on the basis of race, marital status, national origin, religion, disability, age, or sex, there must be a legitimate reason for such treatment. Courts are very sceptical of separation on the basis of national origin, race, or religion, so they apply "strict scrutiny" to such practices, which are usually prohibited. Separation is generally permitted only for groupings based on academic ability or sex in contact sports (as noted above). However, these kinds of separations cannot be automatic and must be for legitimate means. You cannot separate students if doing so is not necessary to support their learning or promote their safety. Students must be allowed to participate with other students without being separated according to their individual needs and abilities. For example, students with limited proficiency in English may be separated in order to receive additional language support during a language instruction segment, but they may not be separated during a math segment unless they require additional support there as well.

Skill 5.7   Recognizing subtle forms of exclusionary and inequitable treatment and strategies to eliminate these practices in the school and classroom

Exclusionary and inequitable treatment can cause great harm to students. Not all forms of such treatment are obvious and readily identified, however. Subtle forms of exclusionary and inequitable treatment are practices that are less obvious than other practices and are not usually written down or codified in school policy. For example, calling on boys more frequently than on girls to respond to questions, encouraging boys more enthusiastically than girls to apply for science opportunities, failing to invite students to attend extracurricular activities on the basis of attention deficit challenges or other identified disabilities, and spending more time providing comments and suggestions on the papers of students belonging to some groups than on the papers of other students—all these are subtle and often unrecognized forms of discrimination.

Additionally, when teachers choose curricula and materials, such as books, wherein all characters belong to two-parent households and are Caucasian, this is a subtle form of communication that implies that one race and one family structure are better than others. Every curriculum must be reviewed to ensure that it is culturally competent and inclusive. There are several steps that teachers and schools can take to prevent subtle discrimination.

Identify subtle inequitable practices within the school and environment, and demonstrate knowledge of ways to prevent such practices.

1. Provide professional development opportunities to ensure that teachers are aware of such practices, and provide resources to address them.

2. Principals should assess classrooms to determine whether subtle discriminatory practices are occurring.

3. Teachers must not make some students "invisible" by failing to call on students whose response may be harder to understand as a consequence of the students' accents or use of language. This practice is both illegal and harmful.

4. Sometimes subtle practices lead to discrimination when teachers use different criteria for providing reinforcement to students. For example, if a teacher praises girls for sitting quietly and boys for working hard, students learn that boys are valued for one thing and girls for another. Thus teachers must be very careful not to create a "highly visible student" problem by praising certain students excessively for specific behaviors and outcomes, to the detriment of other students.

5. Teachers must work to create a classroom community in which each student has an opportunity to try out and take on various roles in the classroom. For example, if teachers have certain students clean up each day and have other students provide tutoring each day, the classroom will learn that certain kinds of kids are good at cleaning and others are valued for their contributions to academics. This kind of stereotyping in assigned roles undermines a classroom community and results in exclusionary practices.

6. Schools have an obligation to protect students from bullying and harassment inflicted by other students for discriminatory reasons. For example, if teachers know that a student is being harassed as "dirty" for having dark skin or a girl is being taunted as "Mr." for having short hair, they have a duty to respond and take action to prevent such harassment.

7. Teachers must make sure that they aren't making seat assignments based on criteria (such as sex, race, spoken language, or the like) that can negatively affect or isolate students. When teachers group students by spoken language, they sentence to isolation students who are limited in English proficiency and also send the classroom community the message that some students need to be kept separate from others.

8. Teachers must use language that is not discriminatory. Relevant precautions include ensuring that pronouns are not used to favor males (i.e., "the Great Man theory of history"), ensuring that students from multiple countries where most people speak the same language are not all labelled in terms of the same area or country of origin (i.e., "Spanish kids" or "African-American kids"), to the exclusion of the many South American, European, Caribbean and/or other countries of origin).

9. Teachers must be careful not to exhibit favoritism by responding to some students, and not others, by use of reinforcements, special opportunities, facial expressions, or other types of body language.

10. Teachers must interpret students' behavior equitably. For example, when a student of one national origin is aggressive toward another child in the classroom, it is important that this not be viewed as physical aggression if another student of a different national origin might be viewed, in the same situation, as still learning to behave in the classroom environment.

11. Classroom displays and wall mounts of leaders should be analyzed to ensure that the pictures don't all represent successful leaders as belonging to a specific ethnic or racial group. Ensuring that classroom posters don't reflect sex-typing is very important in ensuring that subtle forms of discrimination don't exist in the classroom. An example of an objectionable poster is one that depicts nurses and teachers who are all women and doctors and lawyers who are all men.

12. In classrooms for young children with play areas, materials must be reviewed to ensure that they are not representing one culture at the expense of others or subtly favoring any specific group. For example, in a kindergarten classroom with a dress-up area, materials should include clothing and cultural tools that represent various racial and ethnic groups.

Schools can best discourage subtle forms of discrimination by taking an affirmative, proactive approach to ensuring that all children are valued. Schools should provide translators, translated materials, and ensure that visual imagery in hallways and shared areas doesn't favor one group over another, and every school should have a statement posted that expresses the school's commitment to valuing the diversity of its school community.

Sample Test

1. **Which of the following practices illustrates a case where free expression would be limited and might result in disciplinary action against a teacher?**

   A. Discussing a student's decline in academic performance with a community leader without permission.
   B. Discussing the district's publically reported health education policy.
   C. Discussing the upcoming school budget vote at a social event.
   D. Sending an email from home to a colleague encouraging him or her to take a position within the teacher's union.

2. **In order to create an equitable classroom environment free from discrimination, teachers must:**

   A. Ask all students to share their opinion on topics each day.
   B. Review the latest research on managing diverse classrooms.
   C. Treat students respectfully and model the behavior expected of students.
   D. Keep a record of how many questions each child answers.

3. **At the beginning of the school year, a teacher distributes a survey to his students asking them about their extracurricular activities in an effort to learn more about the students in his class who come from diverse backgrounds. This information will have utility in terms of:**

   A. Predicting which students will do well in math and science.
   B. Separating students on the basis of athletic ability, academic support at home, and artistic interests.
   C. Ensuring that instruction is relevant to all children.
   D. Creating leadership circles based on which children regularly practice skills outside the classroom.

4. A student with a disability needs to use a wheelchair in the classroom. The classroom teacher should:

A. Create alternative classroom activities for this student that teach the same skills the rest of the students are learning through other activities at the same time.
B. Create a physical arrangement in the classroom that allows meaningful participation.
C. Put a special table in the back of the classroom for the student's use and comfort.
D. Keep the student next to the teacher's desk so she or he can provide extra supervision.

5. A male teacher named Robin applies to teach at an elementary school. He has 15 years of teaching experience and has received numerous awards for his work with young children. He is not hired for the position, nor are his references checked. When he arrived for the interview, the principal looked surprised and interviewed him very quickly. He later learns that the school has only female teachers. When he approaches the principal to ask about the wholly female staff, he is told that female teachers are better with young children, who require nurturing. Such a statement is:

A. Discriminatory and unlawful.
B. Nondiscriminatory because the school conducted an interview and considered Robin's candidacy.
C. Understandable because young children generally spend more time with their mothers than with their fathers.
D. Nondiscriminatory because the school is a model school where children are succeeding at a higher rate than students in comparable schools nearby.

6. In Oregon places of public accommodation may discriminate on the basis of:.

   A. Race.
   B. Source of income.
   C. Marital Status.
   D. None of the above.

7. A local school notices that its teaching applicant pool is not very diverse and is concerned that people may believe the school hires only Caucasian teachers. In an effort to ensure that no one gets this impression, the school should:

   A. Send a letter to a local African American teaching organization asking for applicants.
   B. Print all teaching advertisements in multiple languages.
   C. Develop a nondiscriminatory hiring policy statement and publish it in high-visibility places throughout the school and in all advertisements for positions.
   D. Refuse to interview any more Caucasian applicants for positions.

8. In order to enroll in a lunchtime enrichment class, students must bring in a letter signed by a parent or guardian. An additional requirement mandates that parents of participating students attend two lunch periods to support the teacher during the school semester. Which of the following efforts should the teacher consider making in order to ensure that enrollment is not inequitable?

   A. Allow parents to pick any two days they wish.
   B. Send material home translated for children whose parents do not speak English, and encourage—don't require—parent participation.
   C. Create a separate program for kids whose parents cannot participate.
   D. The teacher doesn't need to make any additional efforts.

9. During the first two weeks of school, one classroom teacher makes seven referrals for special education. Such referrals generally lead to classification. What policies should the school have in place in order to prevent over-referral?

A. Teachers should ask parents before making referrals.
B. Teachers should ask students whether they think they need extra support.
C. Before making referrals, teachers should document concerns for a period of time and try in-class approaches such as one-on-one support from the teacher where appropriate.
D. Teachers should make referrals immediately upon observing any decline in classroom performance.

10. A new principal has learned that the school she is leading has suffered a sexual harassment scandal and that teachers who feel discriminated against generally don't feel comfortable reporting their experiences. In order to ensure that the work environment fosters openness and prevents discrimination, what should the principal do?

A. The principal doesn't need to do anything. She is not responsible for problems that occurred before she accepted the position of principal.
B. The principal should interview all the teachers to determine whether they have ever felt discriminated against.
C. The principal should create an incentive program for teachers who report discrimination.
D. The principal should post, in teachers' lounges and other visible places, information about how to file a complaint and what to do if a teacher believes his or her reporting is not being taken seriously.

11. According to *U.S. v. Virginia*, an academic program that does not admit students of a particular gender can violate a student's civil rights when:

A. There is a no justification related to the objectives of the program.
B. There is a weak justification related to the objectives of the program.
C. There is a strong justification related to the objectives of the program.
D. All of the above.

12. A teacher is aware that some students who have mastery of content generally do poorly on exams. In an effort to ensure equitable assessment, he should:

A. Add points to the exams on content questions that he knows the students have mastered.
B. Stop assessing students with tests.
C. Develop multiple assessments so that all students have several opportunities to demonstrate their knowledge.
D. Give each child a different assessment on the basis of the child's preferences.

13. Separating students in the classroom on the basis of classifications is generally unlawful. However, there are circumstances in which separation serves a legitimate purpose. Which of the following hypothetical situations represents an acceptable separation of students based on gender?

A. A teacher separates boys and girls for math instruction.
B. A teacher develops a physical classroom arrangement with boys on one side of the room and girls on the other side.
C. A teacher separates boys and girls in the classroom for sports involving physical contact.
D. A teacher separates boys and girls because she believes that gender has an impact on skills and interest in content areas.

14. Subtle forms of discrimination can adversely affect children's self-esteem and well-being. Identify a subtle form of discrimination from among the choices that follow.

   A. Enrolling in professional development to learn more about how to support children in the classroom who have certain learning disabilities.
   B. Identifying children who have mastered concepts and may benefit from additional enrichment.
   C. Suggesting that students meet with the teacher for extra help if they fail a test.
   D. Calling on students who speak clearly and without an accent more frequently than on those with accents, in order to support the flow of learning in the classroom.

15. A female student is regularly teased in the classroom for having short hair and is called "the ugly boy." The teacher is aware of the teasing because it happens regularly. The teacher:

   A. Has a duty to stop the teasing and protect the student.
   B. Doesn't have a duty to intervene because this matter is between children, not between a teacher and a student.
   C. Can ignore the behavior.
   D. Is not required to address non academic concerns in the classroom.

16. The rights granted in the Family Educational Rights and Privacy Act (FERPA) are granted to parents until:

   A. Their child turns 18.
   B. Their child attends a school beyond the high school level.
   C. Their child turns 15.
   D. A &B.

17. A kindergarten teacher wants to make sure that her classroom is nondiscriminatory and values all children. Which of the following is the best thing she can do to ensure nondiscriminatory teaching in her reading center?

   A. Talk with children about the authors before reading a story.
   B. Bring in books by African American authors during Black History Month.
   C. Read bilingual books to children during Hispanic Heritage Month.
   D. Evaluate the books in her classroom to ensure that they represent a wide array of families, ethnicities, and ways of life, and incorporate these books throughout the year.

18. According to the due process clause of the Constitution, the state cannot deprive anyone of life, liberty, or property without due process of law. This clause has major implications for educators because:

   A. Teachers need to ask students for permission before taking something from them.
   B. Teachers are state actors.
   C. Teachers lend property to students in the form of textbooks.
   D. Students use school property each day in the classroom.

19. Prior to suspending a student for a significant period of time, schools must comply with the student's right to due process, because:

   A. Students deserve a chance to be heard.
   B. Teachers could have misunderstood a behavioral problem.
   C. The right to an education is a property interest.
   D. The right to an education is unconditional.

20. Federal law protects people on the basis of which classes?

   A. Race, color, national origin, religion, gender, age, and disability.
   B. Race, color, and national origin only.
   C. Race, color, sexuality, age, and disability.
   D. Federal law does not protect people on the basis of classifications.

21. Protecting students from criticism because of their ethnicity or gender will likely:

   A. Foster confidence and success in minority and female students.
   B. Make all students hyperaware of ethnic and gender differences.
   C. Create an equal learning environment.
   D. Build strong ties between student and teacher.

22. In the state of Oregon:

   A. Sexual orientation is a protected class.
   B. Sexual orientation is not a protected class.
   C. Teachers can be discriminated against on the basis of their sexual orientation.
   D. Courts have not determined yet whether sexual orientation is a protected class.

23. A 20-year-old teacher applies to teach at a local elementary school. After meeting her, the principal suggests that she come back for an interview in a few years. He suggests that she is young and mentions that the children in this school require a teacher who is more "seasoned." This is an example of:

   A. A reasonable criterion for evaluating the needs of a school.
   B. Discrimination based on a disability.
   C. A principal exercising reasonable discretion.
   D. Age discrimination

24. Title III of No Child Left Behind mandates the provision of funding and support and promotes best practices of school districts related to:

   A. Limited proficiency in the English language
   B. Age
   C. Disability
   D. Sexual orientation

25. In a public school in Oregon, an excellent teacher interviews for a position. During the interview, the principal is convinced that the interviewee looks familiar. She generally finds the teacher to be a very favorable candidate and is prepared to make an offer of employment at a second scheduled meeting. That night, the principal goes through her files and finds a picture of a young woman who stole from a local store when she was 14 years old. She recognizes this picture as that of the woman whom she interviewed earlier in the day. As a result, she decides not to make an offer of employment. In Oregon, this decision would be:

   A. Illegal on the basis of the due process clause.
   B. Illegal on the basis of state statutes related to employment discrimination.
   C. Legal
   D. Reasonable because the school has a legitimate interest in making sure children are not around an adult who committed a crime as a juvenile.

26. In the intercultural communication model, students are able to learn how different cultures engage:

   A. In both verbal and nonverbal modes of communicating.
   B. At cultural religious ceremonies.
   C. Between members of their own culture.
   D. In sporting events.

27. If an allegation of discrimination is made in Oregon, the Department of Education must investigate any complaint related to civil rights. If a complaint is well founded, the school must:

   A. Issue an apology for the discriminatory behavior.
   B. Draft a plan to come into compliance with the laws or risk loss of funding.
   C. Publish a statement of zero tolerance for discriminatory behavior.
   D. Close immediately.

28. Which of the following is prohibited by law?

   A. A teacher wearing a religious symbol on a necklace around her or his neck.
   B. A teacher, when asked about a religious symbol, responding that it is a symbol of his religion.
   C. A teacher, when asked about a religious symbol, spending 10 minutes explaining her belief system to the child who asked, along with the reason for wearing this symbol.
   D. A teacher assuming a leadership position within his house of worship, outside of school, on the weekends.

29. If a student is suspended and the parents disagree with the application of this punishment, what recourse do they have?

   A. Parents can grieve the punishment through a meeting with teachers and administrators.
   B. Parents do not have any recourse, because schools have a right to punish children appropriately for unacceptable behavior.
   C. Parents can demand that the child be placed in a new classroom.
   D. Because one has the right to parent one's own child, parents always have the right to overturn a school district's decision about dealing with the child's behavior.

30. A certain teacher rarely calls on a child who recently emigrated from a South American country. His reason for not calling on this student very often is that the student has a thick accent, and the teacher is concerned that the kids in the class, who sometimes can be ruthless, may make fun of him. This teacher is:

A. Discriminating against the child from South America.
B. Creating a safe environment by preventing conflict.
C. Thoughtful in proactively planning for all children in the classroom.
D. Properly addressing the needs of a student with limited English language proficiency.

31. A policy requiring that a parent be involved in order for a student to participate:

A. Is the best way to learn about a student's cultural background.
B. Ensures that the parent and teacher are working together.
C. Allows parents to understand their child's education environment.
D. Can adversely affect children whose parents do not speak English or are illiterate.

32. A well-meaning teacher hands back the graded English essays and states, "As always, the girls in this class did phenomenally well. Your thoughtfulness and ideas are wonderful!" In making this remark, the teacher is:

A. Recognizing kids who have done well, an important thing for teachers to do.
B. Encouraging quality work.
C. Illustrating the creation of a "visible" child which could encourage all the students to believe that girls are better in English than boys.
D. Encouraging girls, which is a very valuable effort for teachers to make.

33. In *Tinker v. Des Moines*, students wearing armbands protesting the Vietnam War were asked to remove the armbands, which they refused to do. The Supreme Court ruled in favor of the students because:

A. Students always have a right to wear whatever they want on their bodies.
B. School is not a special place requiring students to wear approved clothing only.
C. Freedom of assembly allows students to assemble and wear clothing in protest of the war.
D. Freedom of speech prevails, and schools can infringe on this right only if the type of speech threatens the requirements of appropriate discipline in the school.

34. In *Harper v. Poway* the Supreme Court ruled that wearing shirts bearing anti-gay slurs was:

A. Acceptable as long as no curse words were included.
B. Unacceptable because it injured students who had a right to attend school free of injury, and safeguarding that right warranted limiting free speech in schools.
C. A form of free speech protected by the First Amendment to the United States Constitution.
D. Allowable at the discretion of school administrators.

35. According to *Lau v. Nichols*, ESL students (students learning English as a second language):

A. Have a right to language support in school.
B. Should be separated into a class where the curriculum is the same as that taught to English-speaking students but is presented in their native language.
C. Do not have a right to language support in school.
D. Do not have the same right to freedom of expression as English-language speakers.

36. School districts can force staff to retire at age:

A. Schools cannot base a forced retirement policy on age.
B. 75.
C. 85.
D. 65.

37. If students choose not to salute the flag when the class says the Pledge of Allegiance:

A. They can be expelled, because saluting the flag is a part of the civic engagement and development of students.
B. They must leave the room so as to not distract other students.
C. They will be required to stand and salute the flag.
D. They may sit quietly and not participate in the Pledge of Allegiance.

38. **What is the most effective way to encourage open-mindedness in the classroom and expose children to various ways of thinking?**

    A. Show children movies about different cultures.
    B. Celebrate different cultures each month.
    C. Take children on field trips to have hands-on experiences with different ways of life, encountering people who differ in age, ability, religion, and lifestyle.
    D. Develop essay assignments that invite students to write about a peer who lives differently than they do or to tell about a pen pal they have had who lives in a different country.

39. **When creating a classroom community, teachers must be mindful of how they treat female and male students differently. Which of the following is an effective guideline to help teachers achieve this objective?**

    A. Teachers should protect students from having to answer complex questions on subjects that people of their gender are not likely to be comfortable with.
    B. Teachers should monitor their own use of the pronouns "he" and "she" and should ensure that they make equal responses to males and females in the classroom.
    C. Given that many political leaders in history are male, teachers should celebrate only female leadership for a period of time in the classroom.
    D. Teachers should divide the class by gender in accordance with the belief that girls feel more comfortable learning with other girls, and boys feel more comfortable learning with other boys.

40. In order to reduce behavior problems in the classroom and foster a learning environment that incorporates multiple perspectives, teachers should:

A. Incorporate many hands-on and collaborative learning experiences throughout the day.
B. Have a detention corner for children to sit in when their behavior is deviant.
C. Set very clear, strict rules at the beginning of the year.
D. Give each child a day to celebrate herself or himself.

41. When a student with a hearing impairment is in the classroom, the school must provide:

A. A sign language interpreter.
B. No special accommodations.
C. A special classroom for deaf students.
D. A free appropriate public education including an IEP.

42. In order to support positive behavior and on-task, focused work, teachers should:

A. Praise kids as often as possible.
B. Post a rule chart, refer to it frequently, and ensure that any punishments are appropriate and linked to the poor behavior.
C. Develop very strict punishments to deter students from making poor choices.
D. Refer children who misbehave for an immediate evaluation.

43. A student's individualized education program (IEP) is set to be developed on Wednesday. Tuesday evening, however, the child's parents leave a message for the school stating that an unforeseen circumstance will prevent their attending the meeting and requesting an alternative date. Desiring an implemented IEP, the school should:

A. Develop the IEP and begin implementing it.
B. Apologize to the parents but hold the meeting without them.
C. Bring in a child advocate but hold the meeting as scheduled.
D. Reschedule the meeting, because parent involvement is required and essential.

44. A parent is complaining about the lack of specificity in his child's individualized education program. Although the IEP is very detailed, the parent wants it to include even more specific information. Which of the following must be included if the parent requests it?

A. On what dates and where services are offered and how long they will last.
B. A weekly progress-reporting plan for parents.
C. Copies of every assignment completed by the child.
D. A record of questions asked by the student and answers from the teachers and teaching assistants.

45. Parent engagement is something that should:

A. Be fostered by the parent–teacher conference only.
B. Include creatively involving parents in their children's learning.
C. Be measured in terms of the number of parents who volunteer at school activities.
D. Be limited, because education should be under the supervision of teachers only.

46. Subtle forms of exclusionary and inequitable treatment are practices are:

A. Those that favor the best performing students.
B. Are practices that are less obvious than other practices and are not usually written down or codified in school policy.
C. Focus on minority students.
D. Do not occur during school hours.

47. Social understanding and cultural connectedness expand the most when students:

A. Watch a television show about people from a culture other than their own.
B. Read about life in another country in a school textbook.
C. Learn in personalized learning environments with opportunities for multicultural learning.
D. Are separated in terms of level of academic progress in order to ensure that they learn with other students of matched academic ability.

48. Getting to know each student's cultural background and sense of identity promotes:

A. Discrimination
B. Learning and rapport between teachers and students.
C. Favoritism
D. Low educational attainment

49. In classes where there are students who are still learning English, teachers must:

A. Use English only.
B. Separate children with limited proficiency in the English language so that they can practice alone without interruption from English-speaking peers.
C. Use multiple methods to ensure positive communication with every student daily.
D. Send letters home in English only, because all families do better when they interact with English.

50. In order to avoid making incorrect assumptions about students, teachers should:

A. Plan time for interaction in the classroom to get to know all students and their interests and to learn how they like to be addressed.
B. Focus on academic education, not on the development of social skills.
C. As early in the year as possible, classify children into groups based on language, culture, and ethnic background.
D. Celebrate a new culture each month.

51. Students 1ˢᵗ amendment right to freedom of speech:

A. Is protected in all cases.
B. Does not apply during school hours.
C. Can and should be limited if it interferes with the rights of other students.
D. Is absolutely protected by the 1ˢᵗ amendment if it has religious motivation.

52. Diversity in the classroom can be defined:

A. As ethnic and cultural diversity only.
B. As racial diversity only.
C. Broadly, to include ethnic, cultural, gender, socioeconomic, and other kinds of diversity.
D. In terms of educational success and failure only.

53. Every student must have an equal opportunity to succeed. This consideration must be part of lesson planning, because all students must have access to the opportunities and materials they need to be successful. Which of the following statements is true as a consequence of this principle of equal opportunity?

A. Every child should be given a computer to take home for research projects.
B. Teachers should ensure that homework assignments don't require the use of technology that only some students have access to.
C. Homework should not be assigned, because some children won't have additional support at home and thus will be at a disadvantage.
D. Teachers should always stay late to help children complete homework successfully.

54. The concept of invitational education suggests that:

A. Academic success is fostered by clear classroom rules and boundaries.
B. Students should greet each other every morning and practice social responsibility, and teachers should invite effective guest speakers to the classroom as often as possible.
C. Teachers should invite children to join them in a new lesson each day.
D. Teachers are either inviting or disinviting in their behavior toward students, and this has an impact on students' self-concept.

55. When the teacher's observations and a student's classroom performance suggest that he or she is learning effectively, but tests results for the student consistently do not reflect adequate understanding, it is important to consider the possibility that:

A. The student really doesn't know the information and has been cheating during classroom discussions.
B. The student doesn't care about the test.
C. The student is angry at the teacher.
D. The test may not be a valid measure of this student's achievement.

56. A teacher has a class with a mix of students whose first language is English and students who are still very much in the process of learning English. In order to get through her lessons in a timely manner, she generally calls on the English-speaking students to answer questions and explain material. Her rationale is that the English learners will better understand the material as they listen to the answers of their English-speaking peers. This approach to teaching is:

A. Creative and thoughtful
B. Overwhelmingly supported by recent research on teaching language learners.
C. Discriminatory
D. Reasonable because it is difficult to teach students with different levels of language ability.

57. A student misses school on a regularly scheduled school day. His mother sends him in the next day with a note stating that he missed school because his family practices Hinduism and yesterday was a holy holiday that his family spent in prayer. The teacher should:

A. Mark the absence as illegal because it was a regularly scheduled school day.
B. Require the student to stay in at recess for the next week to make up the work.
C. Lecture the student about the importance of attending school each day.
D. Give the student a reasonable amount of time to make up any missed class work or homework, and excuse the absence.

58. A school secretary is required to sit at her desk to answer phones and respond to parents as they come in the door. Her job necessitates a lot of sitting, but she has a physical condition that requires her to stand and walk around regularly. Her employer should:

A. Require her to sit at her desk because this is her job.
B. Purchase a low-cost portable phone to accommodate her need to walk around near her desk from time to time throughout the day, and fulfill her job responsibilities simultaneously.
C. Terminate her employment.
D. Keep her position as it is but overlook cases when she misses phone calls or must be away from her desk, leaving no one to greet visitors to the school.

59. A local school has struggled with a new type of cheating. Students have been writing answers on the inside of baseball caps and scarves and sliding them down to read during exams. Consequently, the school has imposed a school-wide policy forbidding students to wear clothing on their heads. Such a policy is:

A. Reasonable without exception.
B. Reasonable as long as there are exceptions for students who must cover their heads for religious reasons.
C. Unreasonable
D. Reasonable as long as exceptions are made for students who wish to display political slogans on their hats, thus exercising their right to free speech.

60. A student with a developmental disability that significantly impairs verbal and nonverbal communication and social interaction and adversely affects the child's educational performance is provided services in accordance with:

A. The Individuals with Disabilities Education Act (IDEA)
B. State antidiscrimination statutes
C. The Supreme Court ruling in *Brown v. Board of Education*
D. The Federal Employment Discrimination Act

Answer Key

1. A	31. D
2. C	32. C
3. C	33. D
4. B	34. B
5. A	35. A
6. D	36. A
7. C	37. D
8. B	38. C
9. C	39. B
10. D	40. A
11. D	41. D
12. C	42. B
13. C	43. D
14. D	44. A
15. A	45. B
16. D	46. B
17. D	47. C
18. B	48. B
19. C	49. C
20. A	50. A
21. B	51. C
22. A	52. C
23. D	53. B
24. A	54. D
25. B	55. D
26. A	56. C
27. B	57. D
28. C	58. B
29. A	59. B
30. A	60. A

XAMonline, Inc.
25 First Street, Suite 106
Cambridge, MA 02141
P: 1-800-509-4128
F: 617-583-5552

2010

www.XAMonline.com

Oregon Educator Licensure Assessments ORELA

PO#:	Store/School:		
Address 1:			
Address 2:			
City, State, Zip:			
Credit Card #:		Exp:	
Phone		Fax:	
Email			

ISBN	TITLE	Qty	Retail	Total
978-1-58197-596-3	CBEST CA Basic Educational Skills		$19.95	
978-1-60787-174-3	ORELA Administration Examination		$39.95	
978-1-58197-613-7	ORELA Multiple Subjects 001, 002, 003		$59.95	
978-1-60787-173-6	ORELA Protecting Students and Civil Rights in the Education Environment		39.95	
978-1-60787-043-2	Art - Content Knowledge Sample Test 0133		$15.00	
978-1-60787-031-9	Biology 0235		$59.95	
978-1-58197-691-5	Chemistry 0245		$59.95	
978-1-60787-046-3	Earth and Space Sciences 20571		$59.95	
978-1-60787-035-7	Early Childhood/Education of Young Children 020, 022		$73.50	
978-160787-045-6	English Language, Literature, and Composition 0041		$59.95	
978-1-60787-053-1	French - Content Knowledge Sample Test 0173		$15.00	
978-1-60787-039-5	Library Media Specialist 0310		$59.95	
978-1-60787-050-0	Mathematics 0061, 0063		$34.95	
978-1-58197-269-6	Middle School English Language Arts 0049		$59.95	
978-1-60787-051-7	Middle School Mathematics 0069		$59.95	
978-1-58197-263-4	Middle School Social Studies 0089		$59.95	
978-1-60787-052-4	ParaPro Assessment 0755		$34.95	
978-1-60787-040-1	Physical Education 0091		$59.95	
978-1-60787-047-0	Physics 0265		$59.95	
978-1-60787-054-8	PPST I: Basic Skills 0710, 0720, 0730		$15.95	
978-1-60787-032-6	School Guidance & Counseling 0420		$59.95	
978-1-60787-030-2	Social Studies 0081		$59.95	
978-1-58197-718-9	Spanish 0191		$59.95	
			SUBTOTAL	
	1 book $8.70, 2 books $11.00. 3+ books $15.00		Ship	
			TOTAL	

CPSIA information can be obtained at www.ICGtesting.com
Printed in the USA
270716BV00003B/37/P